DOCUMENTS, WORKSHEETS, AND SAMPLE CONTRACTS INCLUDED WITH THIS BOOK

Worksheets (6)

Success Plan Worksheet

Business Name Brainstorming Worksheet

Ideal Client Worksheet

Target Market Worksheet

Mission Statement Worksheet

Business Policies and Procedures Worksheet

Business Documents (7)

Formal Business Plan Template

Invoice Template

UK Invoice Template (with VAT)

Web Design and Development Client Questionnaire

Informal Late Payment Letter

Late Payment Collection Letter

Client Meeting Actionable Items Template

Sample Contracts and Agreements (22)

Virtual Assistant Services Agreement

Freelance Agreement (per hour)

Freelance Agreement (per project)

Canadian Services Contract (per hour)

Canadian Services Contract (per project)

UK Virtual Assistant Services Agreement

UK Services Contract (per hour)

UK Services Contract (per project)

Addendum to Contract

Mutual Release From Contract

Confidentiality Agreement

LLC Membership Agreement

Partnership Agreement

Partnership Dissolution Agreement

Website Design Contract

Project Management Contract

Ghostwriter Agreement

Consultant Services Agreement

UK Consultant Services Agreement

Cease and Desist Agreement

Agreement to Purchase Domain Name

Assignment of Copyright

Editable, fillable versions of all forms are available for purchase on our website:

www.virtualassistantforums.com

or can be copied from the last section of this book

BECOME A VIRTUAL ASSISTANT

THE VIRTUAL ASSISTANT FORUMS GUIDE TO SUCCESS

FOR NEW AND ASPIRING VIRTUAL ASSISTANTS

Become A Virtual Assistant – The Virtual Assistant Forums Guide To Success
2nd Edition

Printed in the United States

Copyright © 2013 Tess Strand and Virtual Assistant Forums

ISBN 978-0-578-11824-6

All rights reserved.

No part of this book or its online counterparts may be reproduced in any form or by any electronic or mechanical means including information storage and retrieval systems, without the prior written permission of the author or publisher except in the case of brief quotations embodied in reviews. For permission requests email legal@virtualassistantforums.com.

Tess Strand
Founder, Virtual Assistant Forums
http:// www.virtualassistantforums.com

Limit of Liability and Disclaimer of Warranty: Our best efforts have gone into preparing this book to help you start a virtual assistant business but of course buying an eNook isn't going to get your business started or make you a successful virtual assistant. The information presented here is provided "as is" - it's your responsibility to utilize the information in the way you see fit. No guarantee of success or profit is written or implied. **The sample contracts and agreement documents and their supporting chapters are not representative of legal advice or instruction. If you have questions or concerns about the validity or binding legality of any of the information or documents included here you should consult a lawyer.**

Trademarks: This book identifies product names and services known to be trademarks, registered trademarks, or service marks of their respective holders. They are used throughout this book for informational purposes only.

Acknowledgements: Big love to Hamid Alipour for his encouragement, and for the countless hours of programming. Gratitude to my first client ever, Laura Dawson, for giving me the opportunity to learn on the fly. Thanks to Janine Gregor for the use of her poem *A Day in the Life of a Virtual Assistant*.

ISBN 978-0-578-11824-6

90000>

9 780578 118246

TABLE OF CONTENTS

INTRODUCTION:
Do You Have What It Takes?

This book has been written with the sole purpose of helping you reach your goal of starting and running **your own successful virtual assistant business**, but just buying a book isn't going to get you from where you are now to **where you want to be**.

<u>You</u> are the only one who can use the information provided here to make your goals a reality. Before jumping in and starting your own virtual assistant business, ask yourself: *Do you have what it takes?*

The Honeymoon Phase

Right now you're probably very excited and eager to get started. You have an endless supply of ideas (and just as many questions). You're full of inspiration and energy to pour into your new business venture, and that's a truly wonderful place to be—harness that energy and make the most of it! But know this: the startup phase in business is similar to the honeymoon phase in a new romantic relationship: You're really only focused on what you want to see. At some point, that blind view of what it's like to be your own boss and live the entrepreneurial dream has to give way to the hard work of actually starting and running your business.

Reality Check

Once you hit that first snag and your hopeful expectation is tempered just a bit, and your energy and enthusiasm start to wane, do you have what it takes to keep pushing toward your goal of business ownership? And once you've got all of the pieces in place, do you have the fortitude and dedication to continue developing and growing your business after your exciting love affair has settled into the routine, mundane tasks of everyday business life? A business, much like a relationship, takes ongoing attention to keep it running successfully year-to-year. A business is not something you can create and then leave on auto pilot.

Another important question: Do you have the skills, talent, and knowledge to provide real, professional services and products to the clients who will need your services? There's a chapter in this book that will help walk you through the process of determining what services you can and should offer, but you must start by being honest with yourself about what you're already skilled to do, and what you're willing to learn.

Dispelling the Myths

Before you get started on your journey to entrepreneurship, it's important to realistically assess whether you have what it takes to not only take that journey to completion (a launched business) but *to success* (a thriving, profitable business). Being in business as a VA has its own unique issues and challenges. It is not a one-size-fits-all business model. There's so much more to it than most people realize initially.

By dispelling the myths surrounding what it means to 'Be a Virtual Assistant' *right now*, you'll gain a more realistic perception of how much time, energy, and money you'll need to invest to get beyond the research and startup phase and into your own thriving VA practice.

Myth #1
All you need to be a virtual assistant is an Internet connection and a computer.
Some people assume that because virtual assistance is a home-based business, it's very quick and easy to set up. While it might be easy to create a home office and acquire the hardware and software that you need to provide virtual assistance services, there's much more to it than that. Later chapters in this book will help you understand and work through much of what is involved, but you should recognize that you will contend with more than where to put your desk. Building and running a business is real work. It's an ongoing process requiring your time and dedication. **Virtual assistance is a profession**. It is *not* a gig, a job, or a hobby.

Myth #2
You can be a virtual assistant in your spare time.
There are many VAs who successfully set up and grow their virtual assistant businesses while working part-time or even full-time jobs. Many of these employed entrepreneurs also have family and other responsibilities to manage while they're navigating the startup process. It CAN be done, but it takes a high level of commitment, as well as excellent time management skills, to create a new enterprise while working outside the home. Some of the most exciting virtual assistant success stories come from those who are juggling it all. And this could very well be YOUR success story, too. But don't make the mistake of going into this thinking it'll involve anything less than an incredible dedication to reaching your goals and investing as much time as possible in making your dreams a reality.

Myth #3
Being a virtual assistant is easy money.
Growing a virtual assistance company requires real work—that's all there is to it. During your business hours, you're either going to be working for your clients or working for yourself, but one way or another, it is work. And it's important to understand that you'll need a healthy percentage of your available work hours to work for yourself. This is time that no one will be

paying you for (but will be an investment in your company). You should expect a good portion of your time will be spent on marketing, keeping your website updated, networking, selling your services, learning new skills, and promoting your business. You may work 8-10 hours a day or more on your business, and only half of those may be billable hours. After reading all of the chapters in this book and completing the relative worksheets and exercises, you'll have a better understanding of just what this means.

Myth #4

A virtual assistant is an employee.

A virtual assistant is a business owner, not an employee. Period. This distinction is a crucial change in mindset and an adjustment you'll learn the importance of when you finally start interacting with clients and potential clients. It's also an important definition to understand for tax purposes. The IRS takes your business ownership (and the relative taxes due) very seriously, and so should you. We'll discuss this in more detail in another chapter.

Myth #5

You don't need special skills to be a virtual assistant.

While it may be true that you are not required or even expected to go to "virtual assistant school" or acquire any kind of standardized certificate to start a virtual assistant business, there is a certain level of knowledge, experience, and ability that you must possess if you expect to be able to maintain a service-based business. Being a successful service provider is serious business. Your clients will expect you to have the talent to back up the services you advertise. Common sense dictates that if people are willing to pay you for something, you'd better be able to deliver.

Myth #6

"Independent" means going it alone.

Just because you're creating your business as a solo entrepreneur doesn't mean you have to do everything by yourself or without support. You'll benefit if you surround yourself with supportive people and rally your biggest cheerleaders to encourage you along the way. The positive influence of someone who understands what you're going through and what you're working toward will help deflect the doubt and negativity cast by people who won't understand why you're pursuing the goal of business ownership or who can't or won't take your dreams of being a successful VA seriously.

Remember, reaching out for support when working toward a difficult goal is a sign of strength, not weakness. The greatest minds and achievers in the business world create networks of support around themselves, and so can you.

Virtual Assistant Forums (http://www.virtualassistantforums.com/) is designed to be an excellent resource not only for the access it provides to extensive, free information throughout the growth and development of your business, but for the all important support, encouragement, and camaraderie you will need as you enter previously unchartered territory. There's even a private (it's not even indexed by the search engines), members-only section called Good Conversation (http://www.virtualassistantforums.com) where you can share personal stories, recipes, fitness tips, WAHM trials and tribulations, favorite books and movies, and so much more – because as all-encompassing starting and running a virtual assistant business is, you'll surely have more to talk about than business!

Knowledge Is Power

You've just uncovered the truth about the six biggest myths related to what it means to own and operate a virtual assistant business. This very blunt introduction is not meant to discourage you; on the contrary, the information you've just read should have the opposite effect. You should now feel empowered, ready to tackle the task at hand: starting your own virtual assistant business.

Here's to your success!

SECTION ONE

Beyond Trust: Ethics = Business Success

Working virtually requires a measure of trust on both the part of the client and of the service provider. While you can put all of your policies and contracts in place to give a legal outline as to how you intend to run your business, nothing speaks louder to your integrity than operating at all times and in all circumstances from an ethical standpoint. This includes operating from 100% honesty with clients *and* with your fellow virtual assistants. Incorporating ethics into your business philosophy and all business dealings will help build trust with your clients and in turn will drive success. Operating from an ethical standpoint is key to the long-term growth of your business.

What Does It Mean to Be Ethical?

According to Dictionary.com, ethical means "*pertaining to right and wrong in conduct.*"

Thesaurus.com offers some synonyms to clarify: "*moral, upright, honest, righteous, virtuous, honorable.*"

While your idea of what is right or wrong may differ from the next person's, there are certain practices that are crucial to incorporate, or avoid, in order to be an ethical virtual assistant (VA).

Tenets of an Ethical Virtual Assistant

- **Honesty:** Present yourself and your business truthfully, including your background, experience, education, skills, and marketable services.

- **Competence:** Only perform tasks for which you are fully qualified. It's one thing to learn a new skill to meet the needs of your clients, but the learning should never be on your client's tab unless you and the client have discussed it openly in advance, and the client has agreed.

- **Authenticity:** Be honest with yourself and your clients about what you can and can't do. Everyone has limitations, and no one expects you to be able to do everything. By being truthful with yourself and clients about your skills and abilities, you help avoid wasted resources, disgruntled clients, and embarrassment. Shine in your work by providing only the services that utilize your best talents.

- **Professionalism:** Present a professional persona during business hours, whether acting on behalf of your clients and their customers and colleagues, or interacting with other virtual assistants.

- **Vigilance:** Protect your clients' interests and information by utilizing effective security measures. This includes having multiple backup systems in place as well as handling sensitive information appropriately.

- **Reputability:** Never use a client's proprietary information, contact lists, or other business resources for personal gain.

- **Reliability:** Uphold your guarantees, agreements, and contracts to the letter.

- **Excellence:** Hold yourself accountable for and take pride in the quality of your work. Set your standards high, and then raise the bar.

- **Integrity:** Accurately and honestly track the time spent on client-related projects, and invoice clients for actual work done.

- **Honor:** Never knowingly participate in illegal activity, either on behalf of your own business or your clients' businesses.

- **Responsibility:** Always perform client requests yourself. If you will be out-sourcing all or part of a project to another service provider, inform your client of this prior to starting work, or cover the possibility of outsourcing from the outset in your contracts.

- **Mindfulness:** Be mindful of your role as a member and representative of both the small business community and the virtual assistant community.

- **Accountable:** Take your responsibility to officially register your business and pay related taxes and fees seriously.

- **Earnest:** Never plagiarize another person's website content or claim any other intellectual property as your own in any way. Write your own website content, marketing materials, and press releases. Plagiarism is the same as stealing and is taken very seriously in the virtual assistant industry.

- **Diplomacy:** Never create negative publicity about another virtual assistant or your clients or past clients in any way via any public medium. There's never a good reason to publicly call someone out, no matter the situation. Handle your grievances in private, with professionalism and decorum.

- **Respectful:** Be respectful of your fellow virtual assistants' thoughts, ideas, opinions, and philosophies when interacting on public forums and social media sites. Remain thoughtful and professional when discussing controversial or deeply personal issues even if you disagree or believe someone to be wrong.

Ask yourself what kind of service provider *you* would want to trust your own business to (as you'll be asking your clients to do) and you'll understand why ethics is a crucial building block in the foundation of your virtual assistance practice.

SECTION TWO
Your Plan for Success: Business Planning

Unless you are trying to secure a loan or other startup funding for your virtual assistant business, a business plan does not have to be a complicated lengthy document full of legalese and financial jargon. It can be more organic in nature and grow along with your business as your experiences inform your decisions and your business goals change. Call it a Plan for Success instead! If you're looking for a casually structured approach to your virtual assistant business plan, this chapter is designed to help you get started.

Of course, if you do need to secure funding for your virtual assistance business, or if you prefer to follow a more traditional, formal business plan format, you can copy and use the Formal Business Plan Template included with this book instead.

Success Plan Exercise

Your plan for success will help give you a sense of focus as you get started on your new business endeavor. And as your business grows and changes, the document can be updated to include new information, new business policies, new plans, etc.

> Copy and use the Success Plan Worksheet
> to help you organize your thoughts and answers
> as you work through the questions below.

Remember, you're writing this *plan for success* for yourself, so you can be as formal or informal as you wish. When you visualize and record the answers to these questions, you're actively participating in the development of your business plan and creating a map to help guide you as you work to realize your goals. Answer every question in each section in as much detail as you can. And don't worry if you don't have immediate or completely clear answers to some of the questions. Once you've worked through each of the chapters in this book, you'll be able to come back and update each response from a fresh perspective!

Section 1: What are your goals?

What do you want to accomplish by operating your own virtual assistance business? Making money shouldn't be the only consideration; what are your short-term and long-term goals for your company?

Section 2: Why are you going into business?

Why do you want to open a virtual assistance practice as opposed to some other type of small business? What does being an entrepreneur/business owner mean to you? How will being your own boss change your life for the better (or perhaps worse)?

Section 3: Who are your clients, and where will you find them?

What kind of people do you want to work with? What industries do they operate in? What business issues, needs, and problems do these people contend with that you can address? Where and how will you network with and market to them?

Section 4: What services will you offer?

What are your marketable skills, strengths, and talents? How do those translate into saleable services that will address your clients' issues, needs, and problems?

Section 5: Where will your business be located?

Will you work from home or hire out either private or communal office space? If you will work from home, where in your house will you set up your home office, and what furniture and equipment will you need to create an effective work space?

Section 6: When will you work?

What days and hours will you be available to your clients? Will you take holidays or personal days? How will you handle sick days? If you are currently working at a job as an employee, how will you handle your employer's needs as well as your clients' needs?

Section 7: How much money will you make/spend?

What will you charge for your services, and how many billable hours a day can you feasibly work? What rates do competing VAs charge? What kinds of things will you have to pay for to get your business started and keep it growing and running smoothly? If you are currently employed and have health insurance and other benefits, how will you handle those costs as a business owner?

Section 8: What is your 5-year plan?

According to the Small Business Administration, over half of all new small businesses will fail within the first five years. What will you do to ensure that your virtual assistant business not only doesn't become one of these statistics, but becomes a true success? **What is your definition of success?**

Section 9: What is your exit strategy?

It's unlikely you've given any thought to the idea of closing your business when you're still working to open it. But this is something you should consider even at this early stage. What are the steps you'd need to take to dissolve your business should you decide to move on to something else or close for some other reason? What's the process to cancel city, state, and federal business registrations and licenses to avoid being charged taxes and fees on a business that's no longer active? How will you close your business bank account? And perhaps most importantly, how would you handle ending your working relationship with your clients?

The bottom line is this: As a small business owner, you can't afford *not* to plan for your business success. Keep your completed plan handy, and use the margins, backs of pages, and new pages to keep it updated as you learn more about your own business goals and desires as a business owner.

As your work through the development of your virtual assistant business plan you can ask questions, get feedback, find resources and tips, and share ideas in the Business Planning section at Virtual Assistant Forums (http://www.virtualassistantforums.com).

SECTION THREE
Setting Up Shop: Your Home Office

Your home office should be more than an extra-room afterthought or a desk pushed into the corner of the family room. This is the place you'll be spending a huge portion of your time now that you're going to be running a business, so it's important to take the location and set-up of your home office to heart. Your office doesn't have to be expensive or elaborate as it's unlikely as a virtual assistant (VA) that you'll be consulting with clients in person there. But the space should at the very least be comfortable, quiet, and private enough to be conducive to productivity.

Where to Put It?

Use the following considerations to determine the best placement for your home office.

Grab a sheet of paper and start by listing three possible locations in your home for your office. The work area should be large enough to be comfortable for you to move around in as needed, and allow enough space for your desk, computer, printer, telephone, file cabinets and any other equipment you anticipate needing. Then check to see whether each location you have in mind meets the following criteria.

- **Wiring:** Are phone and electrical outlets conveniently located so you don't have to worry about tripping on cords?

- **Size:** Is the space big enough to hold your desk, chair, filing cabinet, printer, and all other equipment you need? Grab a measuring tape and make sure.

- **Lighting:** Will the lighting in the room be suitable for working on client projects? If not, what can you do to easily fix the issue? You might consider an additional lamp, lighter window coverings, or brighter bulbs?

- **Walls:** Is there wall space available for a whiteboard or message board where you can organize current projects and schedules, plan out marketing campaigns, or create a vision board?

- **Privacy:** Does the space offer enough privacy so that you can work uninterrupted as needed? If you are easily distracted, consider finding a location that will allow you to close the door.

- **Noise:** Does the location of the space, relative to the rest of your house, prevent you from being bothered by household noise like the television or children playing?

- **Comfort:** How will you feel about spending a large percentage of your time each day in this space? Can you easily create an atmosphere that will be conducive to productivity?

What to Put in It?

You're going to need some basic equipment and furniture to create a functional home office space. Using items you already have in your home is a great way to avoid incurring extra costs during the startup phase. Check sites like Cragslist (http://www.craigslist.org) and Freecycle (http://www.freecycle.org/) to find the items you need at reduced cost or for free.

- **A desk:** Your desk should provide enough surface area to hold your computer, phone, and basic office supplies as well as enough space to be able to comfortably write, organize papers, or open a binder. A desk with storage drawers is even better for keeping an assortment of items close at hand but not in the way.

- **A good chair:** You're going to be sitting in this chair for at least a few hours almost every single day for a long, long time to come. Consider your physical needs when selecting your office chair. Even if you don't have back problems or poor circulation, choose a chair that properly supports your body and encourages good posture.

- **A filing cabinet:** You'll need somewhere to store client files, your own business paperwork and tax information, and any other hard-copy information you collect in the course of business.

- **A phone:** Whether you use a cell phone, a VoIP line like Skype (http://www.skype.com), Google Voice (https://www.google.com/voice), or a land line, you'll want to have a phone in your home office so that you can quickly respond to clients and potential clients. Be sure you have voice mail or an answering machine in place to field after-hours and weekend calls.

- **A printer/fax/copier:** Unless you're specializing in a field that requires high-end printing, you don't necessarily need all of the available bells and whistles, but do treat your printer as an investment in your business. Select a quality model so you don't end up replacing it sooner than expected. And don't forget the paper!

- **A computer:** Again, unless you're specializing in a field that requires a machine with an extraordinary amount of processing power and/or storage space, you don't have to spring for the latest, most expensive computer. Do consider whether you want to work on a laptop or a desktop, a Windows machine or a Mac.

- **An external hard drive:** Your computer is going to store information for your own business as well as for all of your clients and their projects. Imagine the absolute panic of waking up one morning to a computer that simply won't start up. Even if you have a backup computer, what about all of the files or directories you use to get work done for yourself and your clients? Spare yourself the agony by setting up an external hard drive to back up your computer and its contents on at least a daily basis.

- **Online Back-up System:** Consider backing up your files to an online system as well. Once you set it up, it's automatic. In case of a fire or theft, your online files will still be there, not to mention that you can access them from anywhere in the world. Research the reviews online to see what will be the best system for you in terms of storage capacity and price. Here's an article in PC Magazine to get you started: http://www.pcmag.com/article2/0,2817,2288745,00.asp. Then take advantage of the many 30 day free trials that are out there to see which system you like the best.

- **A clock:** Yes, there is a clock on your computer, on your cell phone, and on many of the applications you'll be using, but putting a clock on the wall will keep you aware of the time with a simple glance up.

- **Office supplies:** Don't forget to stock your home office with all the basic office supplies: pens, pencils, notebooks, post-its, printer paper, a calendar, tape, stapler, paper clips, binders, mailing supplies, folders, etc.

Other Items to Consider

If you have the funds and extra space, consider including some or all of the following items in your home office space:

- Whiteboard and markers
- Cork board with push pins
- Secondary large-screen monitor
- Comfortable reading chair with lamp
- Paper shredder
- Hanging shelves
- Blank CDs/DVDs
- Bookshelf
- Backup/emergency power source

Be sure to consider your own business model, services, and potential client needs, and add to this list as necessary. Whatever you do have to purchase for your home office, remember that it will likely qualify as a small business tax deduction at the end of the year, so clearly label and save all of the receipts!

Insurance

Insurance is the kind of thing that you don't really appreciate until you need it and you don't have it. You might think that you are covered by your homeowner's or renter's policy, but you'll need to consult your insurance agent to be sure. Why do you need insurance? Consider that all of your business equipment might be destroyed in a fire or that you may have a burglary in your home. What if a delivery person or even a client was injured while visiting your home-based business? Basically you want to protect your assets in the event that the unthinkable happens. Fortunately, home-based business policies are not too expensive ($300-500 a year), but shop around to get the best rate.

You may be offered a "Professional Liability Insurance" policy, also called an "Errors & Omissions" policy that helps protect the liability of people in the service professions. It's a great deal more expensive than a business insurance policy, and for that reason many skip it.

Check the Work at Home Resources section at Virtual Assistant Forums (http://www.virtual assistantforums.com) for resources and information as well as discussions on everything from buying a new printer to which free online fax service is the most popular.

SECTION FOUR

More Than A Name: Create Your Branding

Your virtual assistant business brand is so much more than a business name, logo, and tagline. Yes, your brand is inclusive of all the things that make your business look good, but when you think about the companies whose brands appeal to you, it isn't just their logo or marketing campaigns that draw you in: It's the whole experience of dealing with them that keeps you a loyal customer. It's the way your interactions with those companies make you *feel* that keeps you coming back.

So, while it's important to have a business name, tagline, and logo that you love and truly resonates with you, it's equally important to realize that every single time you communicate on behalf of your business, online or off, you are effectively creating and recreating, shaping and reshaping your brand.

This means that your blog posts, profiles, comments, and interactions on sites like Facebook (http://www.facebook.com) Twitter (http://www.twitter.com), LinkedIn (http://www.linkedin.com), Google+ (http://www.google.com/+/business/), Virtual Assistant Forums (http://www.virtualassistantforums.com) and even Pinterest (http://www.pinterest.com) all add up to **create your brand**. It also means that your presence at Chamber of Commerce meetings and other local networking events puts you in a position to create a memorable brand experience for those you come in contact with.

At the foundation of it all, *people connect with other people*, **not with a marketing message**. While they may remember your business name or your catchy tagline, they're going to do business with you because they like the way they feel when they deal with you. Maybe you help other small business owners feel empowered to reach the success they crave. Maybe communicating with you on Twitter leaves other Twits with an inspiring sense of can-do.

Whatever it is that's left behind *after* you've communicated, that is the essence of your brand. Keep this in mind as you're working through the brand-building exercises provided in this chapter. Walking the talk isn't just a cliché—*live* your company mission statement, and you'll literally embody your brand as you go out to represent your company and drum up business online and in your own neighborhood.

Creating Your Company Mission Statement

If you want to truly differentiate your business from the multitude of other virtual assistants offering the same services at the same rate, you have to start at the core of your company.

Your mission statement is a short description (*maximum* three or four sentences) of what you do and why, with a nod to your values and/or business philosophy. Your mission statement should be genuine and sincere. Don't trump it up with idealistic statements if they don't really apply to you, your company, or what you can do for your clients.

Copy and use the Mission Statement Worksheet
to help you organize your thoughts and answers
as you work through the questions below.

Answer the following questions and use your responses to craft your company mission statement.

1. What **problem(s)** does your company **solve**?
2. What **pain point(s)** do you **address** for your clients?
3. How is your VA business **unique** from all the other VA businesses?
4. Who is your **target market**?
5. What are your **business goals**?
6. What **values** does your company operate on?
7. What is your **philosophy** as a service provider?

For more inspiration and sample mission statements visit http://www.MissionStatements.com.

Naming Your Business

Naming your virtual assistant business is a very personal process and can be a lot of fun, but many new VAs report that it is also one of the most difficult parts of the startup process. The exercise and information below is provided to help you brainstorm possible names for your virtual assistance business.

Copy and use the Business Name Brainstorming Worksheet
included with this book to help you organize your thoughts
and answers as you work through the exercise below.

- **List *action words* related to the services you will provide**. For example, if you will offer transcription services, you might choose *type, transcribe, write, jot*, etc.

- **List *descriptive words* that you feel apply to you as a service provider.** Examples: *reliable, smart, savvy, virtual*, etc.

- **List *generic business terms* that you might like to include.** Examples: *classic, professional, solution(s), elite, personal(ized)*, etc.

- **List words that you simply *like the sound of*.** Examples: *chic, viva, superb, opal, gauche*, etc.

Don't forget to include the more personal options in your list: your first and last name; your initials; the name of your city, town, or state; the name of your street or neighborhood; and any other words or phrases you think might work well as part of a business name.

Now that you have your list, it's time to start experimenting with options. Combine words different ways. Remove from or add to your list of words as you go. Visit Thesaurus.com (http://www.thesaurus.com) and Wordnik (http://www.wordnik.com) to discover additional related words. For example, *classic* might lead you to *standard, superior, capital, champion*, etc. Keep putting the words together, brainstorming further, and mixing and matching until you come up with several names you like. Now try saying the names aloud. How do they sound? How you feel when you say them?

When choosing a name, be careful not to pigeonhole your business from the start with a name that might later leave you feeling limited. "Carol's Virtual Transcription Services" might describe very well the services you are offering, but it's not a particularly memorable business name, and what if you decide to expand your services or bring in another virtual assistant later on down the road? The same rule applies to "Chicago Virtual Transcription Services" for different reasons: As a virtual assistant, you can and likely will work with clients from all over the world. Don't create the wrong impression with a business name that might imply you only work with a specific, local community.

More tips for selecting your business name

- Choose a name that will appeal to your target market.

- Stay away from slang, jargon, intentional misspellings, or puns that might be misunderstood or, worse yet, might appear to be a mistake on your part.

- Do not use "Inc." after your company name unless you are legally incorporated.

- Choose a name that is concise. Long names are harder to remember.

Once you have one or two names that feel like a great fit, the next step is to find out whether anyone else is using the same name for a similar business. Check online and with applicable agencies for the city and state you live in to make sure the name you've chosen is available for your use.

Visit the Branding Your Business section at Virtual Assistant Forums (http://www.virtual assistantforums.com) to show off your company logo, ask for name and tagline feedback from your fellow virtual assistants, and help other VAs through their branding process as well.

SECTION FIVE
Making It Official: Choosing a Legal Structure for Your Business

Many new VAs wonder whether it's necessary to establish a formal business entity. But choosing not to do so means you run the risk of serious penalties and expensive fines for running a business without the proper registrations and tax payments. Choosing not to follow legally established protocols for business registration also means you're not *really* a business owner.

If you're going to fulfill your dream of being a business owner working for yourself from home, doing it right, right from the first step will allow you to take yourself seriously. In turn, potential clients will take you seriously. Plus, it feels great to see your name and business name on an official business license. It makes the dream all the more a reality.

Use the information and resources provided in this chapter to establish your virtual assistance business correctly and legally. Don't let the paperwork, the cost of filing, and the possibility of local, state, and federal taxes intimidate you. There's no question about it: You can do this! And the reality is, if you want to be a legitimate business owner, you don't have a choice.

Choosing Your Business Structure

The structure you choose for your virtual assistant business will determine the amount of business-related paperwork you will file at the federal, state, and local level; your liability and obligations as a business owner; and the taxes you must pay. To help you decide which business structure will best suit your own business needs and goals, we've briefly outlined the three most common business structures utilized by established virtual assistance practices. Note that your initial choice of structure does not have to be permanent. You can always make a change in business entity if and when your business growth demands it.

Sole Proprietorship

The business is owned and operated by you as an individual. You are solely and personally liable for all debts, obligations, and taxes relating to your business. You are also in complete control of all business decisions and operations.

This is the most common business structure for virtual assistants and other home-based business ventures because it is a simple entity to set up. Depending on your state business registration laws, establishing your company may be as easy as naming your business and obtaining any necessary local business licenses. Be sure to check with your state's business registration office for complete information on cost and necessary forms. To help you learn more about forming a sole proprietorship in your state, we've provided links to websites for the business registration office (usually the Secretary of State) for all US states and territories at the end of this chapter.

You will likely be responsible for paying state business taxes. Most states will automatically send you the necessary tax paperwork at the appropriate times once you have registered your company with the state.

Your business will be responsible for filing the appropriate federal tax paperwork and making relative tax payments to the IRS. Sole proprietors report their business income via their personal income tax returns. You can find more information about how the IRS taxes sole proprietorships, what kind of paperwork is required, and more at the IRS Small Business and Self Employed Website (http://www.irs.gov/Businesses/Small-Businesses-&-Self-Employed/).

Limited Liability Company (LLC)

The business is owned and operated by you alone, or you and one or more people. (The allowed number of involved members and/or other businesses varies by state.) Liability and obligations fall on your company as an entity, rather than you or the individual members of the LLC. Forming an LLC provides the personal liability protection that a sole proprietorship does not.

The process of setting up and registering an LLC is a bit more complicated than the sole proprietorship and varies from state to state, but there are a few common rules: Your business cannot have the same name as another business operating in the same state, and you must include "LLC" or some variation wherever you use your company name. Most states provide an easy online business name search tool that will allow you to research the availability of your chosen company name. When you have a few company names in mind, use Google to search for a business name registry for your own state. This will save time and heartache by eliminating names already in use before you file your paperwork.

For an LLC, you'll also need to file an Articles of Organization (also sometimes called "Articles of Incorporation") for your company. The Articles of Organization is a simple form available through your Secretary of State which includes information about your company such as the company name, who will be running the company, and the registered agent.

The registered agent is the person designated by your company to receive information and documents from the state if your company is ever involved in a lawsuit. (You can list yourself as the registered agent.) You'll then mail the Articles with the appropriate state filing fee to your state's Secretary of State Office. (Links to SOS websites are provided at the end of this chapter.)

You will likely be responsible for paying state business taxes for your LLC. Most states will automatically send you the necessary tax paperwork at the appropriate times once you have registered your company. Note that in some states (New York, California, and Pennsylvania, for example), LLCs are subject to a capital values tax, which can increase your tax burden as a small business. To learn more about necessary forms and the cost of forming an LLC in your state, visit the appropriate link at the list of states provided at the end of this chapter.

A company operating as an LLC can choose to be taxed as a corporation, partnership, or sole proprietor. If you choose to establish your virtual assistance practice as an LLC, it's important to understand these options and file the correct paperwork. Learn more about federal tax requirements for LLCs at the IRS Small Business and Self Employed Website (http://www.irs.gov/Businesses/Small-Businesses-&-Self-Employed/)

You'll find an LLC Membership Agreement
provided for your use should you wish to form
a multi-member LLC at some point
in your business development.

General Partnership

The business is owned by you and your business partner(s). You and your partners equally share all profits, liability, and business operations and responsibilities. *This means that you are not only liable for your own actions within and on behalf of the company, but for those of your business partners as well.*

Partnerships are fairly easy to set up but must be based on a legal document called a Partnership Agreement. The partnership agreement will include information about you and your business partners, the name of the partnership, the purpose of the partnership (what type of business you are in), the principal place of business, and more. Find your own state's link on the list provided at the end of this chapter to learn more about the necessary forms and the cost of forming a general partnership in your state.

Under a general partnership, you will likely be responsible for paying state business taxes. Most states will automatically send you the necessary tax paperwork at the appropriate times once you have registered your company.

Your partnership will also be responsible for filing the appropriate federal tax paperwork and making relative tax payments to the IRS. Members of a general partnership report their business income via their personal income tax returns. More information about how the IRS taxes general partnerships, what kind of paperwork is required, and more can be found at the IRS Small Business and Self Employed Website (http://www.irs.gov/Businesses/Small-Businesses-&-Self-Employed/)

> You'll find both a Partnership Agreement and a Partnership Dissolution Agreement provided for your use should you wish to form, or dissolve, a partnership at some point in your business development.

Understanding DBA (Doing Business As)

When you create a sole proprietorship, the name of your company is your own legal name. When you create a partnership or LLC, the name of your company is the name you enter on the requisite state paperwork. However, if you wish to do business under another business name, you may be obligated to file a DBA (Doing Business As) with your state.

For example, Andrea Smith has registered as a sole proprietor in her state. Legally, the name of her virtual assistance company is "Andrea Smith." But she wants to do business and refer to her company as "Andrea Administration." She must register this "fictitious name" as a DBA or trade name in her state as required.

Not all states require registration of fictitious names, and which government office handles these registrations will depend on where you live.

> To help you track down the information you need relative to your location, we've provided a list of links and information on filing a DBA or trade name at the end of this chapter.

DBA Information and Resources

The information provided below should not be construed as legal advice. We have made every effort to ensure everything listed here is accurate; however, you are strongly advised to confirm the process for officially registering your business in your state or county with the proper authorities before filing any paperwork or processing any fees.

Your Location	Details and Links
Alabama	If you operate your business in Alabama you are not required to, but may choose to register a trade name with the Alabama Secretary of State (http://www.sos.state.al.us)
Alaska	If you operate your business in Alaska, register your business name (http://www.commerce.state.ak.us)
Arizona	If you operate your business in Arizona, you are not required to, but may choose to register a trade name with the Arizona Secretary of State (http://www.azsos.gov)
Arkansas	If you operate your business in Arkansas under a name other than your own full legal name, you are required to file an Application for Fictitious Name (https://www.ark.org/sos/ofs/ docs/index.php) with the Arkansas Secretary of State (http://www.sos.arkansas.gov/)
California	If you operate your business in California under a name other than your own full legal name, you are required to file a Fictitious Name Statement with your local County Recorder-Clerk's Office
Colorado	If you operate your business in Colorado you can register a trade name (http://www.sos.state.co.us/)
Connecticut	If you operate your business in Connecticut under a name other than your own full legal name, you must register a trade name in the town where your business is conducted or register with the Connecticut Secretary of State as a corporation (http://www.concord-sots.ct.gov/)
District of Columbia	If you operate a sole proprietorship, corporation or partnership in the District of Columbia under a name other than your true business name you must register a trade name. (http://brc.dc.gov/)
Florida	If you operate your business in Florida under a fictitious name you must register with the State Division of Corporations (https://efile.sunbiz.org/ficregintro.html)
Hawaii	If you operate your business in Hawaii you can file an application for a trade name (http://hawaii.gov/)

Idaho	If you operate your business in Idaho, you'll need to file an assumed business name (http://www.sos.idaho.gov/)
Illinois	If you operate a general partnership or sole proprietorship in Illinois under a name other than your own full legal name you must register with your local county clerk's office (http://www.cyberdriveillinois.com/)
Indiana	If you operate a general partnership or sole proprietorship in Indiana and are using a business name other than the official name, you must file a Certificate of Assumed Business Name with your county recorder. If you are an LLC you must also file with the Indiana Secretary of State (http://www.in.gov/sos/)
Iowa	If you operate a sole proprietorship or general partnership in Iowa under an assumed name you must file a Trade Name Report with the local County Recorder's office. This rule does not apply to corporations, LLCs that have registered with the Iowa Secretary of State.
Kansas	If you operate your business in Kansas you are not required to register an assumed business name.
Kentucky	If you operate an LLC or partnership in Kentucky you must file a Certificate of Assumed Name with the Kentucky Secretary of State. If you are a sole proprietorship you must file an assumed name certificate with your county clerk's office (http://www.sos.ky.gov/)
Louisiana	If you operate a sole proprietorship or general partnership in Louisiana under an assumed name, you must submit a notarized the Application to Register a Trade Name to your local Parish Clerk of Court office. LLCs must submit the application to the Louisiana Secretary of State (http://www.sos.la.gov/)
Maine	If you operate a sole proprietorship or general partnership in Maine under an assumed name you are required to file a certificate with the municipal or town clerk where your business is located. LLCs must register a Statement of Intention to do Business under an Assumed or Fictitious Name with the Maine Secretary of State (http://www.maine.gov/sos/)
Maryland	If you operate your business in Maryland you can find information on trade name registration and download the trade name application at: (http://www.dat.state.md.us/)
Massachusetts	If you operate your business in Massachusetts under a name other than your own full legal name, you must file a DBA certificate in the town in which you do business.

Michigan	If you operate a sole proprietorship or general partnership in Michigan under a name other than your own full legal name you must file an Assumed Name Certificate with your county clerk. LLCs will register an assumed name as part of the required business filings with the Michigan Secretary of State (http://www.michigan.gov/)
Minnesota	If you operate your business in Minnesota you can submit an Assumed Name Registration to the Minnesota Secretary of State (http://www.sos.state.mn.us/)
Mississippi	If you operate your business in Mississippi you are not required to register an assumed business name.
Missouri	If you operate your business in Missouri under a name other than your own full legal name you must submit a Fictitious Name Registration with the Missouri Secretary of State (http://www.sos.mo.gov/)
Montana	If you operate your business in Montana visit the Montana Secretary of State (http://www.sos.mt.gov) website for the Application for Reservation of Name (http://www.sos.mt.gov/ Business/forms/general/Reservation_of_Name.pdf) the Application for Registration of Assumed Business Name (http://sos.mt.gov/ business/Forms/ABN/01A-Assumed_Business_Name_ Registration.pdf)
Nebraska	If you operate your business in Nebraska visit the Nebraska Secretary of State website (http://www.sos.ne.gov/dyindex.html) for the Application for Registration of Trade Name (http://sos.mt. gov/business/Forms/ABN/01A-Assumed_Business_Name_ Registration.pdf)
Nevada	If you operate your business in using a name that is not the legal business name you must file a Fictitious Firm Name Certificate with your County Clerk (http://nvsos.gov/index.aspx?page=81)
New Hampshire	If you operate your business in New Hampshire visit the Secretary of State (http://www.sos.nh.gov/) website for the Trade Name Registration Forms.
New Jersey	If you operate a sole proprietorship or general partnership in New Jersey under an assumed name you should register with your county clerk's office (http://www.njelections.org/loc_officials_doe.html). LLCs can register an assumed name with the New Jersey Division of Revenue (http://www.state.nj.us/treasury/ taxation/)
New Mexico	If you operate your business in New Mexico you are not required to register an assumed business name.

New York	If you operate a sole proprietorship or general partnership in New York under a name other than your own full legal name you must file a Business Certificate with your County Clerk's Office (http://nysegov.com/). LLCs must register an assumed name as part of their required business filings with the New York Department of State (http://www.dos.ny.gov/)
North Carolina	If you operate your business in North Carolina you'll file a Certificate of Assumed Name (http://www.nccommerce.com/en/Business Services/StartYourBusiness/Forms/) at your local County Register of Deeds Office.
North Dakota	If you operate your business in North Dakota visit the Secretary of State website (http://www.nd.gov/sos/) for Trade Name Registration.
Ohio	If you operate your business in Ohio visit the Secretary of State (http://www.sos.state.oh.us/) website for Trade Name Registration Forms.
Oklahoma	If you operate your business in Oklahoma visit the Secretary of State website (http://www.sos.state.ok.us/) for Trade Name Report.
Oregon	If you operate your business in Oregon visit the Secretary of State website (https://secure.sos.state.or.us/) for Assumed Name Registration.
Pennsylvania	If you operate your business in Pennsylvania visit the Department of State website (http://www.dos.state.pa.us/) for the Application for Registration of Fictitious Name.
Rhode Island	If you operate your business in Rhode Island under an assumed name you may be required to file an assumed name certificate with your city or town clerk and with Rhode Island Secretary of State (http://www. sec.state.ri.us/)
South Carolina	If you operate your business in South Carolina under an fictitious name you are not are required to register with a government agency. Visit the South Carolina Secretary of State (https://www.scbos.sc.gov/) for more information.
South Dakota	If you operate your business in South Dakota visit the Secretary of State website (http://www.sdsos.gov/) for Fictitious Business Name Registration.

Tennessee	If you operate a sole proprietorship or general partnership in Tennessee you are not required to file a DBA. LLCs register an assumed name as part of their required business filings with the Tennessee Secretary of State (http://www.state.tn.us/sos/)
Texas	If you operate your business in Texas under an assumed name must file an Assumed Name Certificate with your County Clerk's Office. LLCs must ALSO file an Assumed Name Certificate with the Texas Secretary of State (http://www.sos.state.tx.us/)
Utah	If you operate your business in Utah under an assumed name you must file a Business Name Registration / DBA Application (http://corporations.utah.gov/)
Vermont	If you operate your business in Vermont, you can register with the Vermont Secretary of State (http://www.sec.state.vt.us/) using the Trade Name Registration Form.
Virginia	If you operate your business in Virginia under a name other than the legal business name you must file an assumed or fictitious name certificate in your county. LLCs must also file a copy of the fictitious name certificate with the Clerk of the State Corporation Commission (http://www.scc.virginia.gov).
Washington	If you operate your business in Washington visit the State Department of Licensing for Trade Name Registration (http://bls.dor.wa.gov/tradename.aspx).
West Virginia	If you operate your business in West Virginia visit the Secretary of State website for Trade Name Registration (http://www.sos.wv.gov).
Wisconsin	If you operate your business in Wisconsin you can file a Registration of Firm Name (http://www.wisconsin.gov).
Wyoming	If you operate your business in Wyoming you can register a trade name with the Wyoming Department of State (soswy.state.wy.us) using the Trade Name Registration form.

The General Legal Issues section at Virtual Assistant Forums (http://www.virtualassistant forums.com) is a great place to discuss the various business entities and get your business registration questions answered.

SECTION SIX
Your Business Bank Account

A s with any business, when you're operating a virtual assistance practice from home, you'll need a business bank account. It's important to differentiate business funds from personal funds for many reasons, and the only way to effectively accomplish that is to set up and maintain a separate bank account for your business.

Business vs. Hobby

As far as the IRS is concerned, you can deduct expenses for a business, but not for a hobby. Keeping business finances in a business bank account gives your business a distinct advantage in this case: How many people you know keep a separate bank account for their hobby? And presenting your business in a professional light isn't just putting on a face for the IRS; it has a positive effect on how your clients will perceive you and your business as well.

Crystal-clear Write-offs and Stress-free Audits

An audit is defined by the IRS as

> "...an examination of an organization's or individual's accounts and financial information to ensure information is being reported correctly, according to the tax laws, to verify the amount of tax reported is accurate."

Being audited is reportedly as scary as it sounds, and it can be an expensive learning curve if you haven't kept your business books clean and up-to-date.

Maintaining a business bank account will not only keep business funds separate from personal funds, it will keep spending separate as well, leaving no question about where payments for things like office supplies, software, your Internet connection, postage, or a subcontractor's services come from.

When tax time rolls around, and especially if you are ever audited by the IRS, you'll have straightforward records to present and an easier time tracking and proving business write-offs.

Good Money Management

Good financial management is the key to ensuring your virtual assistant business has enough funds to operate in the long term. If your goal is to support yourself and your family with your business, you'll need to keep track of every penny, especially while your business is growing. With a business bank account, you're able to keep an eye on running totals for business income as well as calculate business expenses quickly and easily. Tracking revenue and expenses will allow you to consider which aspects of your business require your immediate attention. You'll be able to readily see where you're spending too much money and where you might be able to invest for further growth.

Securing a Loan

It's not unheard of for a virtual assistant to pursue a small business loan for the purchase of equipment, or the expansion of their home office, for example. If you anticipate taking advantage of a small business loan, you'll need to be able to show extraordinary financial organization. Having a well-kept business bank account is an important part of that requirement.

Features of a Small Business Bank Account

There are far too many small business banking options to mention here, but that also means there are a lot of banks vying for you to be their customer, which puts you at a distinct advantage. The more competition for your business, the better your chances of finding a small business banking package that suits your needs, offers excellent customer service and is affordable (or free!) When you're in business for yourself, every dollar counts; don't waste your hard-earned money on avoidable bank fees and egregious penalties.

Consider the following questions when shopping around for a business bank account.

- **Can you get it free?** It's hard to find a truly free checking account option anymore, and even more difficult to find a free business checking account, but it's worth looking around. Be sure to ask specifically about fees for using, or not using, your checks, ATM card, etc.

- **How much do transactions cost?** Most business bank accounts will charge fees starting after a certain number of checks written, deposits/withdrawals made, etc., in a month. Find out how many transactions are free before charges begin, and how much each additional transaction will cost you.

- **Is there a minimum balance requirement?** Every business goes through tough times. It's important to know whether a bank is going to kick you while you're down by penalizing you for being down to your last few dollars.

- **Do they offer online banking?** As a VA who works online the majority of the time, it would be somewhat ironic if you didn't have access to your small business bank account online. And in this day and age, it would be equally ironic if a bank didn't offer online banking services.

Narrowing Your Options

Run a Google search for "small business bank account" and you'll come up with over 17,000 results. Obviously you're not going to sort through them all, so here are a few tips to help you narrow your search and make a decision about where your virtual assistance business will do its banking.

- **Ask around:** Ask fellow virtual assistants where they bank and what they like/don't like about it. Check with your local Chamber of Commerce to see whether it has a relationship with a specific bank. Look online at consumer review sites like Yelp (http://www.yelp.com), MeasuredUp (http://www.measuredup.com), and My3Cents (http://mythreecents.com/) Start your list of potential banks based on positive feedback from others.

- **Make some calls:** Once you have a few recommendations call the branches closest to you to find out what they can offer you as a small business owner. They'll likely invite you in for a one-on-one chat and marketing pitch. It's worth taking the time to visit if they've been recommended to you either directly or indirectly.

- **Take notes:** Ask all of the questions mentioned previously along with any additional questions you may have, and take notes of responses. Close conversations with the contenders by asking what they can do to help make your business finance management easier and more cost-effective. If they don't have a great answer to that question, take them off the list.

- **The short list:** Take the time to visit the remaining banks on your list. You'll get to see how they operate (Is the bank clean? Are the employees professional and courteous?). You'll also get to sit down with someone to discuss what your needs are, what help the bank offers, and how much it's all going to cost. Don't sign up for an account at any one bank until you've taken the time to visit all of the banks on your list and weigh the information you've gathered.

- **Making the choice:** Remember that no matter how big or how small your business is, banking is a service industry. In selecting a bank for your small business bank account, you're trusting another institution to help you manage a crucial aspect of your business. Choose a bank that not only respects where your small business is today but offers services and products that will grow with your business into tomorrow.

SECTION SEVEN
You Are NOT an Employee: Independent Contractors and Small Business .Taxes

As a virtual assistant (VA) operating your own small business, you are officially classified by the Internal Revenue Service as an Independent Contractor (IC) (as opposed to an employee). But the implications of making that distinction clear for *yourself* actually run much deeper than just how often and how much you owe the IRS. As a business owner, you will need to actively work to rid yourself of the employee mindset, especially if you have grown accustomed to working on someone else's clock, at someone else's company.

Shedding the employee mindset is important for two main reasons. First, the IRS will penalize both you and your client(s) if you're paying taxes as an IC but operating essentially as a remote employee. And secondly, you and your clients will approach the business relationship from a much different perspective if you present yourself and behave as a proper IC from day one. A virtual assistant who operates without these lines drawn very clearly risks huge tax liability issues as well as a less than ideal working situation.

It is not your clients' responsibility to know this or to help you make sure you're entitled to your IC classification. Remember, your clients can only interact with you from within the relationship you create and the expectations you provide. **It's up to you as the professsional service provider to set that tone from the start.**

Distinctions of Independent Contractors

There are at least three very important distinctions to be aware of as an independent contractor:

- **No résumés:** A résumé is a tool used by an employee seeking a job. You are a service provider seeking contracted clients. Did you ask your dentist for a résumé before hiring his services? Probably not. When potential clients ask for your résumé, direct them to your online portfolio, send them your brochure and business card, or invite them for a brief consultation to see whether your services are a good fit for their needs, but don't send them your résumé. You are not applying for a job.

- **No references:** References are required by employers during the pre-interview process. When a potential client asks for references, politely mention that you respect the confidentiality and privacy of your clients and never give out their contact information. Then, send them a link to the page on your website where you've provided glowing testimonials from your satisfied clients or point out the portion of your brochure that highlights quips from your happy clients.

- **Business hours:** Employees work when their boss tells them to, and they take breaks on the company schedule. ICs set their own schedules, providing services as and when they choose. That doesn't mean a client asking you to schedule a call with them at X time on X date is crossing any boundaries; your clients will have reasonable requests and suggestions about how and when they can use your help. But as a self-employed business owner, it is your prerogative to decide whether the appointment works for you or not. If your work time with and for a client is solely dictated by the client, you're toeing a very fine line and could be classified as an employee by the IRS.

The above list is by no means exhaustive. To really understand all of the laws governing ICs, you should familiarize yourself with the difference between an independent contractor and an employee:

> "*You are not an independent contractor if you perform services that can be controlled by an employer (what will be done and how it will be done). This applies even if you are given freedom of action. What matters is that the employer has the legal right to control the details of how the services are performed.*"

Taxes

It's exciting getting that first client invoice paid. Unlike a paycheck, you won't have any taxes taken out shrinking your takeaway pay and at first that can be exhilarating. But there's no free lunch, and you'll really need to put some of your revenues away for paying taxes later. As a self-employed person, you actually pay a little bit more than employees do since you need to pay both sides (employee and employer sides) of FICA (Federal Insurance Contributions Act) tax. Let's break it down:

Federal Tax

Just like you have federal taxes taken out of your paycheck, self-employed workers need to pay federal taxes. This will most likely be the largest percentage of the taxes that you pay based on your individual situation. Everyone is different, so do your homework and consult a professional if you are uncertain.

Federal Self-Employment Tax

If you make just $400 your first year in business as a virtual assistant (and let's optimistically assume you're going to make a whole lot more than that), you're going to owe some self-employment (SE) tax to the federal government when you report your income. SE tax covers the Social Security and Medicare deductions that would come out of your paycheck were you still employed at a "regular" job.

SE tax is filed at the end of the tax year using Schedule SE (Form 1040). You can download this and many other forms you might need for free from the IRS website (http://www.irs.gov /formspubs/index.html). The current SE tax rate for self-employment income earned in 2011 is 13.3% (10.4% for Social Security and 2.9% for Medicare).

This means that for every $100 you make, you'll owe $13.30 at the end of the year. If you make $1,000 in 2011, you'll owe $133.00.

If your income is high enough that you expect to owe more than $1,000 at the end of the tax year, you may be subject to quarterly estimated SE tax payments. These are payments that you send in advance, throughout the year, ensuring that if your virtual assistant business makes plenty of money, you don't wind up with an unmanageable tax burden come tax time. Visit the IRS website to read more about SE tax laws, payments, and how to report your income.

The yearly deadline to file federal tax returns and pay any tax that is due is April 15th. You can file your taxes for free online at the IRS website (http://www.irs.gov/efile/index.html).

The IRS website has a section called the Small Business and Self-employed Tax Center (http://www.irs.gov/businesses/small/index.html). Bookmark it for future reference, and spend some time familiarizing yourself with the information available there. It will come in handy at the end of your first year in business as a VA.

Local State and City Tax Laws

In the US, each state (and the District of Columbia, which we will regard as a state) has a unique set of tax laws and regulations governing small businesses and self-employed individuals. Even states like Florida, Washington, and Wyoming that don't levy state income taxes may require business taxes to be paid either quarterly or yearly. When you register your business with your state, you will be provided further details. However, you can find this information on your own by visiting your state's Department of Revenue website.

As you can see, each Virtual Assistant's situation is going to be different based on the personal and family circumstances, not to mention the legal form of business chosen (self proprietor, LLC, partnership, corporation, etc.). As a rule of thumb, however, I put aside one-third of my income to cover federal, state, local, and self-employment taxes. I urge you to consult an accountant or tax professional to determine your tax rates and determine when or if you need to file quarterly estimated taxes so that you don't have an unexpected tax bill.

The Employer Identification Number (EIN)

Even if you do not have, and do not plan to have, employees in your virtual assistance business, you will likely need an Employer Identification Number (EIN). The EIN is a number that uniquely identifies your business to the IRS for the purpose of managing your tax file and tracking your tax payments. When you file various tax forms for your business, you'll use the EIN instead of your social security number. You can quickly and easily get your EIN (https://sa1.www4.irs.gov/modiein/individual/index.jsp) at no cost directly from the IRS website. Or you can download, print, fill in, and mail Form SS4 (http://www.irs.gov/pub/irs-pdf/fss4.pdf)

In order to complete the EIN request form, you'll need to know what business entity you're operating as, your company name, and your personal social security number (SSN). If you're ready now, you can apply for your EIN.

For more thorough information regarding the Employer Identification Number, download Understanding Your EIN (http://www.irs.gov/pub/irs-pdf/p1635.pdf) from the IRS website.

Should You Hire a Tax Professional?

Being in business for yourself brings you face to face with a host of tax implications. It's important to be familiar with both federal and state tax regulations and your relative responsibilities as a small business owner. Even if you choose to pay a bookkeeper and a certified public accountant (CPA) to manage your taxes for you, as a truly empowered entrepreneur, you should have at least a minimal understanding of which tax is owed, how much, and when.

Of course, if you're making enough money to justify the expense (and even if you're not in some cases), it can be beneficial to hire a reputable CPA or tax accountant to work with you come tax time. In many cases, a professional can save you more in deductions than the cost of their services. They'll also be removing the burden of time you would otherwise have to spend preparing and error-checking your federal small business and self-employed tax documents each year. And don't forget that the fees you pay to a professional for services directly related to your business are tax-deductible.

For further discussion of the issues and information presented in this chapter, check out the Small Business Taxes section at Virtual Assistant Forums (http://www.virtualassistantfor ums.com). There, you can ask questions, find additional resources, and join conversations on these topics with other VAs.

SECTION EIGHT

Do What You Love: Determining Your Services

The information and recommendations in this chapter necessarily assume that as a service provider, you are capable of delivering the level of quality your clients expect and deserve. The various tasks and services mentioned here are used only as examples of possible services and/or reflect some of the services currently offered by successful virtual assistants. The selection of services you choose to offer should obviously be reflective of your own skills and abilities.

There's no better measurement for success in business than making a profit doing something you truly enjoy. Better yet is *being your own boss* while making a profit doing something you truly enjoy. Imagine how much more valuable $100 is to the person who earns it under their own company name, on their own time, using skills that challenge and satisfy them! That same $100, earned working at a ho-hum job on someone else's clock, can pay the very same bills, but it's just not *worth* quite as much.

A lot of responsibility comes with running a virtual assistant business, but there are also a lot of perks, not the least of which is being able to decide exactly the type of work you'd like to be doing and create your services menu around that.

There are a multitude of services being offered by virtual assistants, from general administrative services to more specialized niche services. Successful VAs hone in on what they do best and narrow down their services even further to what they love doing most.

The following chapter and accompanying exercises will help you get a head start determining which services your virtual assistant business will offer.

General Administration

Most virtual assistants will provide at least some general administrative services to their clients. Here's a sampling of some general administrative tasks a VA might perform:

- Data collection and entry
- Research
- Record keeping and management
- E-mail and voice mail management
- Customer service and relations
- Mail merges
- Scheduling and calendar management
- Reminders and follow-ups

- Travel arrangements
- Document conversion
- Spreadsheets
- Presentations
- Proofreading
- Contacts management
- Flier creation
- Creating customized business forms
- Project management
- Development and implementation of business systems

The list of possible services is practically endless; it's really only limited by your ability to communicate to clients how a particular service could improve their businesses. Spend some time browsing the virtual assistant forums online to discover even more generalist services common to many virtual assistants. Visiting the websites of established virtual assistants is also a good way to spot trends and get additional ideas for possible administrative services.

Specialized Services

Many virtual assistants also specialize in at least one specific niche and offer these premium services to their clients as well, usually at a higher rate. These skills and services are most often based on a previous career in the respective field, although service providers who are otherwise inexperienced, but serious about entering a new field, can pursue education in a particular area. There are countless niche industries within the virtual assistant profession. Here are just a few of the best-known niches:

- **Real Estate Virtual Assistant (REVA)**
  REVAs provide services to real estate agents and companies. They specialize in creating and managing MLS listings; creating and distributing listing postcards and fliers; creating and managing classified ads; maintaining client contact information; selecting, purchasing, and delivering client gifts; marketing and more. (Learn more about the REVA (http://www.virtualassistantforums.com/real-estate-virtual-assistant-reva-forum) profession from established Real Estate Virtual Assistants at Virtual Assistant Forums!)

- **Social Media Marketing Virtual Assistant**

  Social Media VAs provide services to clients in every industry you can imagine. A Social Media VA might set up and maintain profiles on social networking sites such as YouTube, Twitter, Facebook, Google+, and LinkedIn; create and upload videos to YouTube and Vimeo; manage a client's online reputation, and draft and post material to a client's blog, etc.

- **Virtual Bankruptcy Assistant (VBA)**

  VBAs work with clients in the legal profession. VBAs assist with Chapter 7 and Chapter 13 petition preparation; client intake; due diligence; electronic filing and case management; amendments; and research and analysis, etc.

- **Virtual Receptionist**

  A Virtual Receptionist works with clients in various industries and would primarily provide telephone answering, message taking, call forwarding, and basic customer support services as well as keeping their client up-to-date on the communications he or she has handled on behalf of their company.

- **Virtual Paralegal Assistant**

  Virtual Paralegal Assistants also work with clients in the legal profession and perform highly specialized services such as: preparations for trial and post-trial paperwork and processes; address intellectual property issues related to trademarks and copyrights; do due diligence in respect to various circumstances, and more. Learn more about what it means to be a Virtual Paralegal Assistant from other VPAs at Virtual Assistant Forums (http://www.virtualassistantforums.com).

- **Transcription/Medical Transcription**

  Transcriptionists work with clients in various industries. Any business that utilizes seminars, webinars, video, or audio and wants the recorded information available in text format would work with a transcriptionist. Medical transcriptions work with clients in the fields of medicine and health and have specialized knowledge of medical terminology and HIPPA privacy standards. Bilingual service providers may also provide translation services. Learn more about the Virtual Transcription industry at Virtual Assistant Forums (http://www.virtualassistantforums.com).

- **Virtual Author's Assistant**

  Virtual Author's Assistants work with writers, published authors, speakers, coaches, and others who wish to publish a book. VAA services might include coordinating cover design; layout; securing ISBNs, bar codes, and PCIPs; registering copyright; and registering with the Library of Congress, among other things.

- **Virtual Event Specialist**

  Virtual Event Specialists work with clients in a wide range of industries, from speakers and coaches to corporations—any organization that wants to create and host online events such as webinars, online seminars, live podcasts, and radio shows. VES services offered might include tasks associated with all aspects of organizing, managing, and running the events.

- **Multimedia Virtual Assistant**

  Multimedia VAs work with a broad range of clients. A Multimedia Virtual Assistant might be responsible for podcast production, training, and distribution; radio broad-casting; video production and editing; presentation production; and audio-video syncing.

- **Publicity Virtual Assistant**

  From small businesses and startups to larger companies and corporations, any organization looking to leverage publicity for growth might turn to a Publicity Virtual Assistant. These VAs handle press release writing, editing and distribution; public relations; media pitching; web copy writing and editing; and marketing campaign development.

- **Virtual Speaker's Assistant**

  Virtual Speaker's Assistants work with professional speakers including: motivational speakers, keynote presenters, trainers, seminar leaders, and presenters. These virtual assistants manage a variety of tasks for their clients from responding to, scheduling, and managing speaking opportunities to setting up travel arrangements, to managing the sale and customer service for their clients' products.

Determining Your Services

It's important to remind yourself that you may not have pat answers for something like which services you wish to offer at this early stage in your business' development. As you're getting your business up and running, you'll want to start out offering services you are certain you can deliver at the highest quality, services that will wow your clients, help fill out your business, and build your sense of confidence as a business owner. As you become more experienced and have the opportunity to work with more clients on a wider range of projects, you'll naturally begin to develop a sense of what you truly enjoy doing, what you don't like doing, and what you're interested in learning more about.

To start your virtual assistant business with a strong foundation, the following exercise will help you begin to hone in on a core set of services with which to launch your company. Grab a couple sheets of paper and a pen.

Step 1: List

List your skills, qualified experience, talents, and strengths. This list can be as long as you want it to be. Include everything you can think of that might lead to a marketable virtual service. If you're good at it, write it down. Maybe you're a great listener, you can type 85 WPM, you have an eye for detail, you're a stickler for correct spelling and proper grammar, you have excellent time management skills, you're a whiz with Photoshop. Whatever it is you consider an asset, add it to the list.

Step 2: Delete

Just because you're good at it doesn't mean you should turn it into a service. If there's something on your list that you can't imagine working at every day, and loving it at the end of the day, get rid of it.

Step 3: Branch out

Start a new sheet of paper. List the remaining skills, experience, talents, and strengths across the top of the page, then break each item down into potential services you could provide or markets you could serve with that asset. Remember you're going to be working virtually, so your services should suit that business model. For example, if you're good at organizing things, you could build a service around organizing receipts (which your clients could send you in the mail), or managing large amounts of data (which could be done online).

Other Considerations

What if a client or potential client approaches you with a request to handle work you don't actually enjoy or are otherwise not qualified to perform? This is an issue faced by successful virtual assistants from time to time, so it's worth addressing.

Rather than turning a client down entirely, many service providers will rely on fellow VAs to handle tasks that they don't enjoy or are not skilled to complete. In these cases, they'll either offer the client a referral or discuss subcontracting the work to their colleague on behalf of the client. Developing a network of professionals with skills and services that complement your own is an excellent way to ensure that all of your clients' requests are addressed, whether those requests speak to what you like most or not. Another option is to simply set a higher price point for services you excel at but don't necessarily enjoy performing.

Remember, whatever services you decide to offer initially, your list of services is not set in stone. You can and will revisit this list many times during your career as a virtual assistant, so don't be too hard on yourself. The goal now is to come up with a package of services you can provide that will help your clients build better businesses and find more time to do the work they love as well.

Chances are, you'll have questions about some of the services you are considering offering, and there are also potential services you might wish to offer that haven't even occurred to you yet – visit the <u>Determining Your Services</u> section of Virtual Assistant Forums (<u>http://www.virtualassistantforums.com</u>) to learn and discuss further the myriad services your fellow VAs are considering. You'll also find Niche Virtual Assistant Forums at VAF where you can discuss specific specialties within the VA industry. Broach niche-specific issues, share resources, and ask questions related to being a Real Estate Virtual Assistant, a Virtual Transcriptionist, a Virtual Bookkeeper, a Virtual Paralegal Assistant, and even a Virtual Assistant Subcontractor (yes, some VAs do successfully specialize in working for *other* virtual assistants!)

SECTION NINE
Crunching Numbers: Setting Your Rates

One of the most difficult aspects of setting up a service-based virtual business can be determining how much to charge for which services. You can't just pull a number that sounds good out of thin air. If you guess too high and price yourself out of the market, you'll never contract any clients at all. And if you guess too low, you may run yourself out of business before you even have a chance to get things going.

Many new virtual business owners, plagued by uncertainty and anxious to land that first client, err on the side of caution and set their fees exceptionally low, or use huge discounts or free trials to try to entice clients. This approach often backfires though, as it tends to attract bargain shoppers or clients who are solely focused on the cost of services rather than the value those services provide. The truth is, whether the quality and value are there or not, people automatically attach a lower perceived value to a product or service that is priced too cheaply.

Instead of devaluing your own services from the very start, you need to arrive at a profitable rate with consideration to what clients in your niche are willing to pay. Notice we didn't use the term "livable" to describe the rate you're aiming for. However much you love doing what you do, you can't afford to under-price your skills. A successful business needs to make a profit. **You're in business to make money.**

Money can be a difficult topic. It's a mental hurdle that can be very hard for some to get over, to the detriment of business growth and success. The idea of charging for and actually making decent money providing a quality product or service that brings *the service provider* happiness and satisfaction is somewhat of a foreign concept, especially to someone in the early stages of entrepreneurship, struggling to break free of the employee mindset.

As a business owner, you have to get used to dealing with and talking about money, and fast. The sooner you come to accept and honor the fact that you are in business to make money, the better. Freelancers who give the slightest hint of guilt or uncertainty over their advertised rates diminish the perceived value of their services and leave themselves open to clients who will drag the business down with haggling and negotiation.

Naturally, you're also in business to espouse all of the ideals and philosophies you hold true. That's a given for most entrepreneurs. But what isn't a given is the ability to confidently command a profitable rate for services. Of course, in order to shore up that confidence, you have to offer services you can consistently deliver on at 100%. It also necessitates being aware of what other service providers in your niche are charging for the same level of service. Specialty and in-demand services are always going to command a higher price point than more general administrative services.

Because your market is global, your rate is not necessarily dependent on your location or your local business economy unless you're planning to market strictly to local businesses (But why limit yourself when the world is literally full of potential clients you can easily "meet" online!).

Two main issues come into play when determining your rates:

1. How much your level of skill and knowledge **is worth** to your potential clients
2. How much you need to charge to make **a profit**

Market Value

It can be hard to put a definite number in answer to the first question. To find the answer, you'll need to do your research. Visit the websites of established and successful virtual service providers who offer the same services in the same niche. You'll begin to get a general idea of what the going rate is for your specialized services and general administrative services alike.

Making a Profit

Responding to the second issue is a little easier. It's just a matter of crunching the numbers.

As a self-employed business owner, you're now responsible for the cost of your own health care, your own taxes, your own vacation and sick days, your own business supplies, and the cost of any training, software, hardware, utility bills, and other expenses. You're going to need money for advertising and professional services such as accountants and web designers. And don't forget things like living expenses, rent, food, and fun – you're working for yourself so you can have a life too, right? You get the idea: It's a long list. All of these expenses have to be factored in to help you determine how much you need to charge to make a profit.

You'll also need to look at how many billable hours you will have available in an average week, as well as how much vacation, sick, and holiday time you anticipate needing away from your business.

It's a lot to consider, and it results in a pretty big equation. Fortunately, there's a very handy little calculator (http://freelanceswitch.com/rates/) prepared by FreelanceSwitch for entrepreneurs just like you that will help you quickly and easily experiment with the numbers. Enter your figures into each of the fields provided. If you aren't sure of a particular answer, make your best guess. Click the "Calculate Rates Now" button at the very bottom to get the results. Use this number to help you gauge the validity of the range of rates you may already have in mind after visiting your fellow virtual assistants' websites.

Raising Your Rates

If you're just getting started, it's of course too early in the game for you to think about raising your rates. You'll want to get a full practice of ideal clients in place before you consider raising your rates, but at some point, it's going to be time to charge more. Maybe you're expanding your business to include a team of service providers, or perhaps you've learned a lucrative new skill and want to charge a premium for the new service you're going to add. Or, it's entirely possible that you have gotten so incredibly good at what you do that you're literally turning work away and see an opportunity to charge more for the increasing demand on your ever-more valuable time. Whatever your reasons are, the time will come, likely more than once, for you to raise your rates.

But how do you raise your rates without losing your existing clients? The fact is, you can never guarantee that a client or two won't part ways with you over a rate increase. But by keeping rate increases reasonable, timely, and justified, the client who is already sold on the amazing value you bring to their bottom line is not likely to walk away. And the client who does abandon the relationship over a 5 or 10% rate increase probably didn't place the same kind of value on the investment they made in their business by working with you.

To avoid this problem at the outset, some virtual assistants will make an annual rate increase of a pre-determined percentage part of their contract. This introduces the knowl-edge of regular rate increases early on, but it also locks you in to whatever your contract states.

When you've determined that you're ready to raise your rates and you've come to a decision about how much more to charge, list all of the value-adding changes that have gone into your business in the last year (new software, new services, expanded team, etc.). You'll use this information to "sell" the new rate to your existing clients. But the goal is not to justify the rate increase; this is not a defensive maneuver. This is business, and you don't justify, apologize for, or edge around a rate increase.

Draft a professional but friendly notice to all clients, informing them of the date, amount, and value-adds behind the rate increase. Be sure to allow enough lead time to let your clients process and adjust to the rate change. A minimum of 30 days notice is generally expected. 60 or even 90 days is more generous and shows your clients that they are still your top priority, even as your rates are increasing. Explain clearly how and when the rate increase will be implemented. By focusing your notice on the value additions and how they will benefit your clients, you keep the tone of the message from sounding defensive, or worse, desperate (which a rate increase should never be).

If you've given enough notice, there will be time to follow up once more and remind clients of the change a week or two before the new rate takes effect. You may even use the opportunity to encourage them to take advantage of the old rates by sending in those projects they've been holding off on. Just be sure to honor the old rate for the duration of the project(s), even if that work extends into the billing cycle when the new rate takes effect.

Raising rates ranks right up there among the most stress-inducing aspects of running your own service business. But don't let the nervous anticipation that you're likely to experience keep you from moving your business forward into more profitable territory. Many virtual assistants have approached raising their rates and come out the other side stronger for the experience, and better paid!

Setting and raising rates can be tenuous and leave you feeling uncertain no matter how long you've been in business. Find even more information regarding rates and billing as well as the support and encouragement of your fellow virtual assistants in the <u>Rates and Billing</u> section at Virtual Assistant Forums (<u>http:// www.virtualassistantforums.com</u>).

SECTION TEN

A Strong Foundation:
Your Business Policies and Procedures

Many of the business policies you'll put in place will come about as the result of a learning experience and will be implemented after the fact. We hope the information in this chapter will help you avoid some of those cases of learning the hard way. In business-geek it's called "risk management" and "operational success." We'll just call it good business sense.

Copy and use the <u>Business Policies and Procedures</u>
<u>Worksheet</u> to jot down notes and policy ideas in
response to the questions below.
Then keep it handy and add new considerations
as you work through the rest of the book.

Policies and Procedures Exercise

When developing policies and procedures for your own virtual assistant business, these are some questions to consider.

How will you handle the new client intake process?

You'll need to invest some extra care and time in some clients who are not familiar or entirely comfortable with the concept of working with a virtual assistant. What procedures can you put in place to help your client make this transition with ease? What procedures will you put in place to ensure your investment of time and energy in the new client does not go to waste should they default on a payment? Will you do a credit check on new clients? Of course you will require a contract, but will you require a deposit? How will these issues play out in your own business policies?

How will you communicate with your clients?

Will you be available by phone, cell, e-mail, instant messenger, fax? Which of these methods will best facilitate and honor your own personal needs and business goals while fulfilling the needs and expectations of your clients? Will you answer the phone any time during business hours, or will you only take calls at pre-scheduled appointments? How many times a day will you check and answer e-mail? Will you bill for time spent on e-mails and phone calls?

When will you be available to your clients?

It's important to have clear business hours in place so that your clients know when they can get in touch with you, and for your own sake as well. If you don't want to work weekends or evenings, don't answer the phone or e-mail during these times. Remember, clients can only assume you are available to them at odd hours if you respond to them at odd hours. That doesn't mean you can't work at odd hours, if you choose; that is your prerogative as a business owner. But it is important to establish and maintain boundaries that work for you, especially because you'll be working from home. If you do accept a rush request outside of regular business hours, will you charge a premium? Which national, personal, or religious holidays will you take off? How will you handle vacation time, sick time, or family emergencies?

How will you manage your time?

In order to successfully grow your own business while at the same time tending to your clients' needs, you need to become a master at time management. You have a specific number of hours in any given day available to fulfill your roles as business owner, consultant/service provider, and perhaps parent, spouse, friend, relative, employee (if you're also working at a job outside the home), etc., as well. You'll want to be able to give your clients accurate turnaround times for their projects (deadlines you can comfortably meet) while still taking care of your own business and personal needs and responsibilities.

How will you handle projects you are not qualified for?

This is where having a network of other virtual assistants to call on can be of great benefit to your business. When a client asks you to complete a task you are unable to personally fulfill, for whatever reason, will you find another VA to help? Will you spend your own time learning the skill so that you can help your client and add another service to your menu in the process? If you do pass the work on to another VA, how much information about the third party will you share with your client?

How will you invoice your clients?

How often will you invoice your clients and on what terms? Will you invoice every week, every two weeks, once a month? Will you be working on an hourly, pay-as-you-go plan, or will your clients be working with you on a monthly retainer? Will payment be due before or after the fact? Will you require payment on receipt of the invoice or within a particular time frame? If you are invoicing hourly, are there any circumstances in which you would require partial or full payment in advance?

What types of payment will you accept?

Will you accept PayPal (http://www.paypal.com), Square (http://www.squareup.com) money orders, checks, direct deposit, Intuit Payment Network (https://paymentnetwork.intuit.com/) or some other method? Or will you accept all of the above? If you accept checks, how will you ensure you're paid on time and in full? If you accept PayPal or another system that charges fees per transaction, how will those costs be handled?

How will you handle late payments and defaulted accounts?

A client who pays you a healthy deposit in order to start work with you is an unlikely candidate for unpaid invoices, but it does happen. Whether you choose to take deposits and advance payment or not, chances are at some point in your career as a virtual assistant you'll deal with a late or altogether unpaid invoice. Are you willing to take regular payments against an overdue invoice? Better yet, what kind of late payment penalty, and/or incentive for early payment will you incorporate into your business policies to discourage the practice of ignoring the due date on your invoice?

How will you raise your rates?

If you're good at what you do, at some point demand for your services will outrun supply. Or perhaps you've updated your skill set in order to make new, high-end services available to your clients. It's at this stage that you can start to think about raising your rates. But how will you do that without losing your current clients? What percentage will you raise your rates, and how often? Many virtual assistants have a yearly 2-5% rate increase written into their contracts with a promise of 30-90 days notice/reminder for their clients as a courtesy. What policy will work best for your own business?

How will you handle sensitive client information?

You're going to have access to plenty of personal and financial client data. How will you securely receive, store, and manage this information? How can your business policies help ensure your own credibility and your clients' privacy?

How will you ensure secure data storage?

Regardless of the nature of the information, as far as your clients are concerned, every file, folder, and e-mail they send you is important. What will your business procedures be regarding data storage and archiving?

Are there any other potential issues you can think of that deserve to be written into your policies and procedures? Allow for the fact that as you and your business grow together, you'll fine tune your own expectations as a business owner and can relatively fine-tune and add to your business policies and procedures. The questions provided above comprise a starting point to help you get familiar with the kinds of things that new virtual assistants may miss during the excitement of the startup phase, and often pay a price for later on.

Put It into Practice

A final word of cautionary advice: Many new virtual assistants are so desperate to work with their first client that they'll compromise on or even completely forego many of their own most important business policies and new client procedures for the sake of landing the contract. More often than not, this leads to disastrous consequences, and often means the end of the working relationship because of misguided expectations, unpaid invoices, or both.

Don't sacrifice all the time and effort you're putting in to create and launch your virtual assistant business only to let all of the careful planning crumble around you on the hope of a single contract. You're building these business policies for the sake of your own long-term success. If you expect to be in business a year from now, do more than skim over the suggested thinking points listed here; give them your attention, write them out, use them in your business—in short, implement them in practice, not just in theory. Take them seriously and expect your clients to do the same. Any client who doesn't respect your business policies in the first place and asks you to eliminate just one for the sake of the contract is NOT an ideal client. Ideal clients understand that you are a business owner and a profes-sional service provider. Ideal clients will take you seriously—but only if you take yourself seriously and operate on clear-cut business policies and procedures.

Visit the Policies and Procedures section of Virtual Assistant Forums (http://www.virtual assistantforums.com) to discuss further, ask questions, and find additional resources and information and learn which policies and processes your fellow virtual assistants are talking about.

SECTION ELEVEN

Why You Can't Afford to Work Without a Contract

Disclaimer: This chapter and any of the related print-outs should not be construed as legal advice. This chapter stresses the importance of contracts in business dealings and elaborates on a few specific aspects you may wish to include in your own contract. If you have questions or concerns about information presented here, you should seek professional legal advice.

Too many virtual assistants launch their businesses and start working with clients without contracts in place. Their excuses range from "It's too expensive to hire a lawyer to look my contracts over" to "I didn't have time..." and "I didn't realize I would need one." It's only after they get burned by an unscrupulous client, usually not getting paid for their hard work, that they finally put a contract in place. That can be an expensive lesson to learn.

The $1,330 Question

Imagine you're working with a new client. You've been updating the client's website, creating a newsletter, editing blog posts, and answering customer service e-mails. You're thrilled with the workload and happily work your way through the to-do lists, which come on an almost daily basis. You're racking up the hours. After two weeks and 17 hours at $35 per hour, you send your first invoice for $595 to the client along with a friendly reminder that payment is due on Net 14. That gives your client two more weeks before they must reconcile your invoice.

You continue on with the work requests, all the while assuming the client is going to make good on their balance due. The client continues to send plenty of work, and you're excited about what this could mean for your business. At the next two-week mark, you send your second invoice, this one for $735. The previous invoice is due today, but your client, who is usually readily available by e-mail and IM, is nowhere to be found. Over the next few days, your client continues to be mysteriously absent. There are no more work requests, but there are also no payments being made on the work you've already done.

Your client owes you $1,330. It starts to become crystal clear that you're not going to get paid. You finally reach your client on the phone only to be told the check is in the mail, your invoices never arrived, the work wasn't up to par, or the client is having a cash flow problem. The myriad excuses drag on for another two weeks, and you have no recourse because you have no contract and no deposit.

So, the $1,330 question is this: **Can you afford to do business without a contract?**

If you do the math, you'll get your answer. Spending thirty minutes to find sample contracts online (or better yet, use the ones included with this book!) is a whole lot less expensive than $1,330. Factor in having a lawyer look over those same contracts, and it's still cheaper.

Put simply, **you cannot afford to operate your business without a contract**.

Pitfalls of Not Using a Contract

At the risk of sounding like a broken record: **when there's no proposal or contract in place between you and your client, <u>you're choosing risk</u>**. Small business is risky enough with a huge percentage of new small businesses closing before they even reach the end of their first or second year; why invite unnecessary risk into your own business?

- **Risk of not getting paid:** If you don't stipulate your payment policies and relative business procedures to your clients from the very beginning, you set yourself up for the scenario described at the beginning of the chapter. How are you going to answer the $1,330 question?

- **Risk of mismatched expectations:** A contract clarifies what your client can expect from you and your services, and it clarifies what you expect of your client. This is particularly relevant if you have a team or if you outsource some of your projects to other service providers. When expectations are left unaddressed and unwritten, you can anticipate issues later on.

- **Risk of scope creep:** When you've clearly outlined the project scope in your contract, you have a framework to refer the client to when he or she comes back to you for "quick little changes." In these cases the client may expect the changes to be made gratis, but if your contract specifies the cost of updates to the project outside the original scope, you can bill fairly for the work without confusion or concern that the client might come back to you with questions about the invoice.

- **Risk of confusion:** Again, if you don't tell your client what to expect, from billing policies to office hours, you can assume an issue will crop up eventually. Your clients can't read your mind. They don't know, for example, that you don't work evenings and weekends unless you tell them. They won't know that their rush request on a Saturday is going to cost a 50% premium above their regular rate. It's not enough to share this kind of information over the phone or in an e-mailed response the day the issue comes up. It should be clearly covered in your contract.

No contract is a guarantee of payment, nor is it a guarantee that your client will uphold other aspects of the work agreement. But not having a contract at all leaves you with nothing to prove there was ever an agreement in the first place should you need to implement your late payment policies, invoice for additional work outside the original scope, send a deadbeat client to collections, or take legal action in small claims court.

Your Business, Your Contract

It's your business; you should use your own contract. A contract helps clients see you as a professional, and they'll be more likely to treat you as one if you've presented them with your own contract. A contract doesn't have to be exceptionally long or filled with legalese. As long as it clearly details the responsibilities and expectations of everyone involved and is signed by all parties, it is a legally binding document.

Choose a standard template (like one of those provided for you with this book) and edit it thoroughly to suit your own company language and policies. Your contract should inform your client of the scope of work, the cost for services, and the proposed time frame for projects (when applicable). Don't forget to include things like payment terms, deposits, late fees, and any other conditions relative to money. The contract should also outline your client's responsibilities in the working relationship such as making available the deliverables necessary to perform your work. Obviously your contract will be worded to protect your interests in the business relationship, but it should also address potential issues on your client's behalf such as missed deadlines and mistakes.

> Read through the numerous sample contracts provided, and adapt them for your own business use as needed. Included are Virtual Assistant Agreement, Freelance Agreement (per hour), Freelance Agreement (per project), Addendum to Contract, Assignment of Copyright, Website Design Contract, Partnership Agreement, Partnership Dissolution Agreement, Project Management Contract and Ghostwriter Agreement.

When They Won't Sign

If your potential client won't sign the contract, be tactful but cautious. Most clients are business owners themselves and understand that a contract is a standard requirement for doing business. When a potential client doesn't want to commit to a contract, even if the objection is related to only one or two of your clauses, respond with a brief explanation of why that particular portion of the contract is necessary. Make it clear that it is not negotiable. If you're still met with resistance, politely inform the client that you are unable to commence the working relationship. Invite the client to get in touch again when they've had time to reconsider. **The bottom line is: If the client won't sign, you won't work.**

This is admittedly easier said than done, especially if it's your first potential client or the project is particularly lucrative. Passing up work for lack of a contract is another of those difficult but necessary things that must sometimes be done when you're running a business.

When Clients Want to Use Their Own Contracts

Regardless how carefully you've drafted your contract to be sensitive to the client's point of view, you may encounter potential clients who insist on using their own contract to cement the business relationship. When this happens, ask to see a copy of the contract and the clauses they're adamant about. If you have any question that the additional clauses will leave you or your business at risk, consult a lawyer before including them. If the points they're insistent on do not infringe on or compromise your own policies, it's reasonable to consider incorporating these terms into your own contract. There may be room for compromise without sacrificing your own stance. If it's a relationship you don't want to walk away from, broach the possibility of merging your business policies into their contract.

On the other hand, if a client simply insists that you must sign his contract, completely for-going your own legal document, think twice. Give serious consideration to the message you're sending as a professional service provider if you agree. If you concede on such a major aspect of the business relationship, where do you expect to stand in other matters?

Important Clauses

There are many variations on the freelance contract/proposal. Some are based on a per-project model, where the contract applies to a single project. Some are per-hour or retainer-based contracts, or both. Whatever the circumstance, there are a few specifics you must include if you're going to adequately protect yourself, your company, and your client's interests in the final written document.

Client deliverables

This section outlines exactly what the client is responsible for providing, along with deadlines for receipt, in order for you to complete the work being commissioned.

Fees and other charges

This section details the when and how much of deposits and specifies what is refundable and what is not. Include incremental payments (when applicable), date and amount of final payment due, and additional expenses the client will be responsible for. Don't forget to mention the details of your late payment penalties.

Changes to scope of work

This section explains that if your client changes the project considerably after work has begun or requires excessive edits or changes after the project has closed, you reserve the right to revisit and re-quote the cost of the project.

Exit clause

This section stipulates what happens if the client decides not to follow through with the project after work has commenced or otherwise makes it impossible for you to complete the project (i.e., not providing deliverables on the agreed-upon schedule). This clause should include stipulation of payment for all work-to-date and clarify non-refundable deposits. It should also address what will happen if you are unable to fulfill your obligation to the contract.

Basic Contract Outline

Following is a very basic outline of the sections you will find in most standard contracts:

1. Overview of purpose of contract
2. Parties involved (virtual assistant and client), including addresses, phone numbers, etc.
3. Date
4. Definitions: glossary of frequently occurring terms in the document, such as "Client" and "Consultant"
5. Term: period of validity of agreement
6. Pricing (if for more than one service/product, listed separately)
7. Pricing adjustment (annual rate increases, rush fees, etc.)
8. Responsibilities of provider: extended description of services being provided
9. Responsibilities of client: detailed description of deliverables required for completion of work
10. Payment terms
11. Confidentiality clause
12. Dispute and arbitration process
13. Termination of agreement
14. Terms of renegotiation/renewal of contract
15. Names and signatures of all parties involved

Be sure to make good use of the Virtual Assistant Contracts section at Virtual Assistant Forums (http://www.virtualassistantforums.com). It's a great place to get feedback on your contracts and clauses, ask questions, and find additional resources.

Confidentiality Agreements

As a virtual assistant (VA) working closely with your clients on the growth and development of their businesses, you'll have knowledge of and access to your clients' personal, business, trade, and financial information. As a result, there must be an established level of confidentiality between you and your clients.

In order to put this issue to rest so that information can be shared freely without concern, your client will likely ask you to sign a confidentiality agreement or NDA (Non-Disclosure Agreement). This document offers assurance that your client's confidential information and ideas will remain strictly private. When you sign an NDA, you provide a guarantee that you will not divulge any client information without that client's express written consent for any reason other than a legally court-ordered subpoena.

There are two common types of confidentiality agreements. One is written solely for the protection of the client's interests, ideas, and information. The other is written with both the client and the service provider in mind. Some virtual assistants utilize the latter in their own business dealings and will offer their signed NDA to clients as a show of their commitment to confidentiality.

Note though that many clients and companies will present their own NDA to be signed. Though these forms are fairly standard, you should always thoroughly read anything that you are asked to sign, and have a lawyer look it over prior to signing if you have concerns. It is a generally accepted practice among service providers to agree to sign a client's confidentiality agreement (as opposed to insisting on the use of your own).

It's interesting to note a movement among some service providers in various industries to refuse to sign NDAs altogether. You'll need to decide for yourself whether you feel comfortable signing one or not, but you should realize that if you refuse, you will very likely lose the client in the process. (For more information on declining to sign NDAs, run a Google search for "Why I won't sign your NDA.")

> Copy the Confidentiality Agreement provided
> to see what kind of information is included in a
> standard agreement. Feel free to adapt the
> use of this form for your own needs.

Who Will You Partner With? Defining Your Ideal Client

P a g e | 65

SECTION TWELVE

Who Will You Partner With?
Defining Your Ideal Client

One of the top concerns of startup virtual assistants (and even some who've been in business for a while) is the difficulty of finding clients. It's pretty obvious that without clients, a virtual assistant business simply cannot survive, so why do some VAs seem to have an endless stream of new clients and projects while other VAs struggle for months without a single client?

Without a doubt, consistent marketing to your target market is crucial to success. Well-established VAs have carved out a portion of every single business day to focus on growing their own businesses by reaching out to and interacting with the industries they service. But ongoing evangelizing to your niche market is just one part of the answer to "How do I find clients?" Referrals are a great source of new clients as well, but referrals can only come if you have a client to brag about you in the first place.

Successful virtual assistants have all gone through essentially the same startup process, but one of the key differences between success and failure is that successful virtual assistants have taken the time to *clearly define their ideal client*.

Think about the last time you planned a dinner party. You prepared: You read recipes, created a menu, planned your food from appetizers to desserts, chose the wine, even labored over the table setting.

Now imagine, after all that planning, what would have happened if you went to the grocery store without a shopping list, blindly walking the aisles, tossing random items into your shopping cart.

It would be next to impossible to fulfill your vision for the dinner party, and you'd have wasted a lot of time and countless resources in the process.

Too many virtual assistants approach building their clientele with the same aimless approach, blindly trolling for clients without a well thought-out definition of what kind of qualities they want in a client. But you are going to make that client "shopping list" right now...

> Copy and use the Ideal Client Worksheet to help you organize your thoughts and answers as you work through the questions below.

Ideal Client Exercise

Answer the following questions to help you define your ideal client. It's all right if your list doesn't come together immediately. The truth is, your ideal client profile can (and should) change as you become more savvy about your own business goals and what you enjoy most about the work that you do. As you encounter new experiences, different people, and various work styles, you'll learn from them and will be able to continually fine-tune your vision of the ideal client.

- **What type of industry would you enjoy being involved in?** For example, do you enjoy working with creative types (photographers, artists, authors, choreographers), technical types (programmers, lawyers, doctors), or people who help others better their lives (life coaches, business coaches, educators)? The possibilities are truly endless, and it's OK to list more than one industry. The goal is to narrow your focus and pinpoint which industries will be fulfilling for you.

- **What size business do you want to work with?** There are vast differences working with startups and entrepreneurs versus small to medium-sized businesses, and larger corporations. For example, with a small business, you'll likely be dealing with one or two decision makers whereas a large business or corporation is likely to have a board of directors. What other differences can you infer that will help you make a decision about what your ideal is? Don't worry if you don't readily know the answer to this (or any other question) right away. As you move forward with your business, your experiences will inform these opinions and ideals.

- **At what stage of business development is your ideal client?** Are they in startup mode or well established? What aspects of one or the other stage appeal to you?

- **What style of communication do you prefer?** List the adjectives that describe the communication styles that resonate with you.

- **What level of involvement in his/her own business does your ideal client have?**

- **What are your ideal client's demographics?** Consider elements like age, location, gender, marital status/family status, education, etc.

- **Does your ideal client have experience working with a virtual assistant?** is he or she familiar with virtual assistance? Does the client currently work with one or more VAs? If so, how will you fit into the scenario?

- **How does your ideal client view the role of a VA in his/her business?** How do you fit in to the client's business? Are you a team leader? Part of a team? An assistant? A virtual business partner?

Who Will You Partner With? Defining Your Ideal Client

P a g e | **67**

- **What kinds of services does your ideal client require?** What sorts of projects do you envision working on? What pain points will you address and solve for your ideal clients, and which services will come into play?

- **How many hours a month does your ideal client need?** Think about how many billable hours you have available in a week or month, then consider how many hours you'd ideally like to be devoting to a single client. Assume you have more than one client; don't allocate all of your available hours to any one client, however ideal.

- **How savvy is your ideal client** when it comes to the Internet, technology, etc.?

- **What else is important to you?** What other attributes do you envision in an ideal client?

Use your answers to the questions above to help you clarify who your ideal client is.

Remember, you can come back to the worksheet to update your answers and revise your definition at any time. In fact, it's likely you'll do so at least once during your first year in business.

It's important to realize that not every potential client will be a good match for you, your services, your values, or your business philosophy. By taking the time to define your ideal client and better understanding your own expectations as a business owner and service provider, you'll possibly save yourself the headache of partnering with a client that isn't a good match. And with your "shopping list" in mind, you'll no longer be casting your net without direction.

Ultimately, being aware of who your ideal client is, and making decisions about who to work with based on that definition, makes you a better service provider because you'll be working with clients and on projects that fulfill your goals and match your values. It's your recipe for long-term success.

Keep It Positive

Don't add things that you *don't want* to the list. There's no sense putting your energy toward something negative. For example, if you start to write a negative "*My ideal client doesn't micromanage,*" turn it around as the positive "*My ideal client understands that I am a skilled professional, capable of managing the project from start to finish.*"

Join the ongoing conversations in the Virtual Assistant / Client Relations section of Virtual Assistant Forums (http://www.virtualassistantforums.com) to discuss and share ideas on everything from new client best practices to more serious client relations issues.

SECTION THIRTEEN
Taking Aim: Defining Your Target Market

It's a pretty simple concept: **Once you know who you want to work with, it's easier to find them.** You know who your ideal client is, so now it's time to pinpoint the industries where you should target your marketing efforts.

No business can afford to waste money, and yours is no exception. Small businesses in particular need to make sure that each dollar spent and every hour invested are wisely utilized. Defining your target market means you know exactly where to aim your marketing efforts and can avoid unnecessarily wasting money and resources.

Which approach to a direct-mail marketing campaign do you think will get the best results?

> Sending out fifty brochures to a random selection of small businesses
>
> OR
>
> Sending out fifty brochures to companies you know can utilize your skill set, understand the value of your services, afford your rates, appreciate your background, and appeal to your desire to work with clients in a specific industry

Of course, sending your brochures to a selection of businesses you've pre-determined to be an ideal target market is going to bring a better return.

Defining your target market is a similar exercise to defining your ideal client, but on a broader scope. You're looking now at the industry level in order to confirm, first of all, that there's a need for your services there, and second, to find specific methods of reaching into those markets via marketing, advertising, and networking.

It's not enough to identify that you're planning to service "small businesses." Small businesses vary widely. How would you even begin to determine where to aim your marketing strategies?

> Copy and use the Target Market Worksheet
> provided to record your thoughts and answers as you
> work through the exercises below.

Use the following questions to help you pinpoint your target markets.

- **What specialized services are you offering?**

- **What problems do your services solve for potential clients?**

- **Which industries will best benefit from the use of your services? (and/or) Which industries are you interested in servicing?**

- **What is the average income for businesses operating in these industries?** Use Google, the Small Business Administration website, and other resources to locate some figures. It's important to determine whether the intended market can sustain your business. Only keep viable industries on your list.

Do Your Homework

Now, research and record possible advertising and networking opportunities for each viable industry.

- **Where do professionals in X industry spend time online?** (Include industry-specific forums, blogs, membership sites, social media sites, professional networks, and other types of online communities in your search.)

- **What newsletters, magazines and other feeds or publications are professionals in X industry reading and subscribing to?**

- **Are there any offline events, conferences, conventions, retreats, etc. that professionals in X industry attend?** (Look for events you can either travel to locally, are worth considering long-distance travel to attend, or that you can participate in in some other way such as advertising, sponsoring, or providing promotional items for goody bags.)

- **How else can you share your message and business information with your target audience?**

If you've thoroughly answered all of the questions above, you've defined at least one target market and should have some good leads for implementing your marketing strategy.

SECTION FOURTEEN
Getting Their Attention: Marketing and Networking

Having a registered business and well-stocked home office simply isn't enough to connect with and contract the clients that will be the lifeblood of your virtual assistant business. You've got to get your business name out there to get people talking about and interested in your services. And you've got to give them something to talk about.

If you're working a full- or part-time job outside the home while setting up your practice, it might seem difficult to find time for business-related activities, but you should plan to spend a *minimum* of one hour each day devoted to marketing your business.

Ideally though, you'll be spending the same amount of time on actively marketing and/or networking each business day that you would otherwise spend working with clients. For example, if you're anticipating 3-5 billable hours a day working for clients, you will ideally invest 3-5 hours a day now in finding, marketing to, and contracting those clients.

Ultimately, the more time you spend on establishing and growing your business, the sooner you'll have an active client base—and the sooner you'll find yourself in a position to cut back hours or even quit that full-time job.

Get started networking and marketing your business with the following methods.

Local Networking

Your Chamber of Commerce

Your local Chamber of Commerce can be a wealth of information, small business resources, advertising opportunities, and in-person networking events. By networking locally, you not only build your local connections but your confidence as you field questions about what you do and how you do it. Interacting with other Chamber members will allow you to fine-tune your promotional message so that you're able to quickly and confidently respond to your potential clients' questions without hesitation.

Run a quick Google search or use the ChamberFind (http://www.chamberfind.com/) online chamber directory to locate your own Chamber of Commerce. Note that most Chambers of Commerce require a one-time or yearly membership fee to participate. The fees can generally be written off at the end of the year as a business expense and are a worthy investment in your growing business.

Business Networking Groups

Use local business directories and Google to identify local business networking groups to join. Get on their mailing lists so you'll be notified when the next networking meeting will take place and can plan to attend, prepared. These meetings are usually a gathering of small business owners and entrepreneurs interested in exchanging business cards and discussing opportunities to connect further as well as offer and receive referrals. Ideally, you'll meet with business owners who may need your services.

Get Out There!

A few more ways to make the most of your local business community:

- **Give talks.** If you're comfortable speaking in public, consider creating your own event for local small business owners. Share your knowledge and expertise in a way that immediately benefits those you've invited to the event and you're likely to garner respect as well as make a number of important business connections. Be sure to create an event that isn't just an in-person advertisement for your services. Give your attendees real information they can implement to better their business right away. Include branded handouts and worksheets along with your business card or brochure.

- **Attend and/or participate in conventions and expos.** Attending conventions and expos created for your target market is a great way to build visibility for your virtual assistant business. Participating as a speaker or presenter or setting up your own booth will also help you build credibility. Be sure to go prepared with plenty of business cards, brochures, and any promotional items (branded pens, notebooks, t-shirts, etc.) you can hand out.

- **Build rapport.** People connect with others they know and trust. Generate trust by building rapport with your newfound network. Mail greeting cards and thank you notes to those you've met. Follow up with messages of gratitude for their time and an invitation to connect on the social networks you participate in. If you see a news article, blog post, or event announcement that you think might benefit one of your new connections, forward it in a brief, friendly e-mail that includes your branded e-mail signature with your company name and website URL.

Visit the Networking Offline section at Virtual Assistant Forums (http://www.virtualassistant forums.com) to learn what your fellow VAs are doing to get more local recognition and business and generate fresh ideas for how you can do the same!

Online Networking

Facebook

Facebook (http://www.facebook.com) is easily the largest and most popular social network. With millions of people using it to connect to their friends, family, and favorite companies and brands, Facebook is a good place to situate yourself and your business. But don't confuse the use of a site like Facebook as a bulletin board for your announcements and promotions. Social networks are, first and foremost, social. Your approach to marketing your virtual assistant business here should take this into account.

Create your business page on Facebook and keep it updated with important information for and about your target market. Share your expertise and skills without blatant self-promotion to make the most of your presence. Including a link to your Facebook page in your e-mail signature is a great way to build your Facebook network.

LinkedIn

LinkedIn (http://www.linkedin.com) is another popular social network, but it differs from Facebook in that it is mainly business-oriented. Join LinkedIn to network with and connect to other business owners directly or via the many industry-related and niche groups featured on the site. Use your LinkedIn profile to promote your business, list your skills, talents and services, and collect testimonials from your clients and colleagues.

With more than 50 million registered users in 200 countries, this professional networking site enables you to build yourself to expert status in your field by contributing to the discussions and answering the questions posted by other users.

Twitter

Twitter (http://www.twitter.com) is a social media phenomenon. With status updates (called "Tweets") limited to 140 characters, users are forced to get straight to the point. Collect a legion of "followers" on Twitter by scanning for users whose tweets include keywords relative to your target market, skill set, and interests.

A dynamic and interesting social media network, Twitter lets you have real-time conversations with other business owners and individuals, follow trending topics as they're being discussed, and reach out for immediate advice, feedback, and opinions. While it does take some time to develop a network of followers on Twitter, it's an investment that drives traffic to your website or blog and lets you get to know other entrepreneurs.

The same rules apply to Twitter as any other social network: Join the site prepared to engage first and foremost. Don't just start tweeting 140-character advertisements for your company. Those tweets certainly do have their place in your timeline, but use them sparingly.

Pinterest

Pinterest (http://www.pinterest.com) is described by Wikipedia as *"a pinboard-styled social photo sharing website"* While the evolving social sharing platform was considered very 'new' until recently, and did not cater to the business market, that changed in November 2012 when the site launched business pages. Creative marketers, taking note of the incredible popularity of Pinterest, are discovering ways that Pinterest can be used as an effective marketing tool.

As Pinterest business pages are still relatively new, we'll steer clear of offering specific tips for use of the site and recommend Googling recent articles on *Create a Pinterest Business Page* or *How to use Pinterest for Business.* Pinterest has huge potential to drive traffic back to your own website or blog so it's worth exploring.

However, it's important to realize that because the site is foundationally visual, allowing users to 'pin' images and videos to their virtual bulletin boards, pinning and sharing on this site should not be approached the same way you would interact and share links on Facebook or another less visually-oriented social network. Here, pictures speak louder than words.

Google+

Google+ (http://www.google.com/+/business/) is search giant Google's foray into social networking. Although relatively new compared to Facebook and Twitter it has quickly become another important staple of a small business' social marketing arsenal. Much like Facebook, users can have both a personal and a business page (the link we've provided here is to Google+ for business).

Use your Google+ business page to grow and engage your market much the same way you would on Facebook by posting valuable content your audience will be inclined and inspired to +1, share, and comment on.

As individual users add your company to the 'circles' they've created on their personal Google+ page your impact and interaction with them increases. Unique to this platform, even further engagement is possible with the Google+ Hangouts feature which allows you to network live (as your business page) in a video conference with individual users.

As with any of the other social networks, it's important to be mindful of your target market's demographics, preferences, interests, etc. and be respectful of the fact that when an individual user connects with your Google+ business page they are telling you they are interested in learning more about your company (but they are not interested in being spammed.)

Discuss Facebook, LinkedIn, Twitter, Pinterest, Google+ and more in the Social Media Marketing section at Virtual Assistant Forums (http://www.virtualassistantforums.com). Learn more about the how (and why) of setting up your profiles at the various social networking sites, ask questions, share and discover resources to help you more effectively manage your own (or your clients') social media accounts.

Forums

Forums such as Virtual Assistant Forums (http://www.virtualassistantforums.com) are the original social networks. Participating in the conversation and making the most of all that your forum memberships have to offer is an important part of your Internet marketing plan— IF you take advantage of the opportunity. Here's how.

- Keep your audience in mind.
- Establish yourself as an expert.
- Get involved and stay active.
- Brand everything from your forum profile to your forum posts.
- Utilize forum features such as blogs, signatures, etc.

You may think that the only people reading your posts on the forums are other VAs, but your potential clients are eavesdropping, too. Take advantage of the great SEO a large, well-indexed forum is going to have by posting helpful, well-articulated replies that highlight your expertise and skill set.

Remember to be professional, friendly, and outgoing when participating in forum conversations. Use your forum posts to set yourself apart and *shine as a leader*. In short: Post as if your business depends on it!

Your forum posts are a powerful marketing tool. Use them to make an impressive mark in the virtual assistant industry and in your specific niche.

Download the Free Guide to Making the Most of Your VAF Membership from Virtual Assistant Forums (http://www.virtualassistantforums.com) to gain more insight into how forums (and all of your online interactions) help you build your brand, gain recognition and expert status among your virtual assistant peers, AND get you clients. (You'll also find a handy free **Getting Started as a Virtual Assistant Workbook** available for download on that page!)

More Marketing Ideas

Postcards

Create a postcard with a compelling offer or call to action, and mail it to businesses in your target market. Include your logo, company tag line, and the information recipients will need to get in touch with you. Note that postcards can be an expensive option when you consider the cost of design, printing, and postage. Even if you create the design yourself, it could be cost-prohibitive to send out postcards unless you have a very targeted list of prospects or leads.

Check the General Marketing and Networking sections at Virtual Assistant Forums (http://www.virtualassistantforums.com) for more extensive resources and information.

E-mail Marketing

The Internet has enhanced connectivity, and e-mail marketing has been proven to reel in potential clients with a good pitch. Your distribution list should be populated with people who have directly contacted you through an enquiry form on your site and/or signed up to receive information from you via e-mail. E-mailing too often or sending marketing e-mails to anyone who didn't opt in to receive information from you is considered spam and is likely to turn off your prospects entirely. Use this marketing tool with respect for those on your list. There are numerous online e-mail marketing services that make it quick and easy to upload your list of prospects and create and send a branded e-mail template. While there is almost always a fee to use these services, you can usually sign up for a free trial to get the hang of the software and see whether it's a good fit for your needs.

Visit the Newsletters and Email Marketing section of Virtual Assistant Forums (http://www.virtualassistantforums.com) for more extensive resources and information.

Press Releases

Write a press release about new developments in your business and publicize it via the online press release distribution services (usually for a fee, but there are some good free PR sites out there as well). Remember that a press release should not be mistaken as a chance to overtly advertise your virtual assistant business. Your press release should contain truly newsworthy information. Use the main body of your press release to announce new partnerships, services, or upgrades to your company. Use the "About" portion of your release to share general information about your company. Keep the press release interesting and newsworthy, and it may even get picked up by your local paper. Many virtual assistants have been invited for local newspaper, radio, and television interviews as the result of properly written and distributed press releases.

One of the best resources for press release writing and distribution information is the Learning Center at PR Web (http://service.prweb.com/). There, you'll find articles, whitepapers, and even webinars on how to write, optimize, and effectively distribute your company's press releases.

You can also discuss effective press release tactics, find free press release distribution resources, and post your press release draft for feedback in the Press Releases section of Virtual Assistant Forums (http://www.virtualassistantforums.com).

Search Engine Optimization (SEO)

Think of the Internet as a giant, digital, modern-day Yellow Pages. This is where a huge majority of business owners and entrepreneurs (your potential clients!) go to find what they need when they want to buy a product or service. If your site isn't optimized, or if it isn't indexed by the search engines, it's nearly impossible for your target market to find you easily online. Invest some time in learning the basics of SEO. Implement things like image tags, correct keyword density, page titles, SEO-friendly URLs, and good navigation on your website to increase the SEO of your website. Work to increase the number of backlinks to your website by making sure you've included your website URL in all of your social networking and forum profiles and signatures, then start submitting your site to the better online link directories. SEO is an ongoing process, and there is a lot of competition for virtual assistant industry-related keywords. When considering your own keywords, hone in on a specialty, location, or some aspect of your niche to help your potential clients find you online.

One of the best resources for learning SEO basics is Google's own SEO Starter Guide. Regularly updated with new information, the most recent version of this guide (as of this writing) is available for free downloading (http://static.googleusercontent.com/media/www. google.com/en/us/webmasters/docs/search-engine-optimization-starter-guide.pdf)

Also visit the General Marketing and Networking section at Virtual Assistant Forums (http://www.virtualassistantforums.com) to get your SEO questions answered!

Article Marketing

Writing and publishing informative articles based on your expertise and niche is a great way to increase your status as an expert while building valuable backlinks to your website. Submit your articles to online article directories. To get the most out of your articles, choose high-quality, well-maintained article directory sites. Don't publish your article in too many places; choose the best two or three article directories only. Be sure to include a professional bio and a link to your site in the author information section or byline. The more valuable information you publish online, the more recognition you'll receive among your peers and potential clients.

The Article Marketing section at Virtual Assistant Forums (http://www.virtualassistantforums. com) provides information on which articles directories are best, how to optimize your articles, and more.

Video Marketing

Creating an informational video about your business and services is a great addition to your marketing arsenal. Write a script, and either record yourself sharing the information or set the written text to stock images and music. For maximum exposure, include the video on your website and share it on sites like YouTube (http://www.youtube.com), blip.tv (http://www.blip.tv/) and Vimeo (http://www.vimeo.com). You can also create informational videos for your target market. For example, explain how to use a particular software, or review a product or service. Post these videos on your blog. A few more tips: Keep videos short and to the point. Be yourself; be authentic. Enunciate and make sure your audience can hear you, and your message, clearly.

Referrals

Your best leads for new ideal clients will come from existing clients and colleagues who already know what you do and how beneficial it is to work with you. The potential clients they send you are worth their weight in gold because they arrive already evangelized and ready to make the most of what you have to offer. When you've built a reputation for trust and professionalism with even one client, that client will happily send referrals your way. And don't be shy about coming right out and asking satisfied clients and colleagues for referrals.

When you do receive a referral, even if it doesn't lead to a signed contract, send a sincere, handwritten thank you note to the referring client. Let the client know how much the recommendation of your company and services means to you. You might even consider providing clients with a little added incentive to send their own colleagues your way by offering a special discount or other gift for clients who send referrals. Whatever type of referral incentive program you put in place, make sure that it serves your own best interest and doesn't undercut your own business growth.

Creating Your Marketing and Networking Plan

As you can see, there are myriad ways to effectively market your business both online and off as well as numerous opportunities for local networking as a small business owner. This chapter only touches on the most basic possibilities. The best marketing and networking plan will draw from many of these and will include experimentation with new and different ways of reaching out to and connecting with your target market.

Don't be content to set up your social networking profiles and go to one or two local events. Consistent marketing is a crucial part of growing your business. Use the information in this chapter to create your own initial marketing and networking plan. Keep track of how much time you invest in each method every month and note what works (and what doesn't).

Again, you should invest a bare minimum of one hour every single. Ideally, you'll devote more time than that in the beginning as you grow your fledgling virtual assistant business.

When you're ready to explore all of these possible marketing and networking directions, visit the Marketing Your Virtual Assistant Business section at Virtual Assistant Forums for discussions, resources, tips, tricks, hints, and tools you can use in your own business marketing plan. (http://www.virtualassistantforums.com)

SECTION FIFTEEN

Your Virtual Assistant Business Website

In the age of iPads, smart phones, and wi-fi, you can safely assume that your target market is online and using the Internet to do business. As a business owner and virtual service provider, it's absolutely crucial that you maintain an online presence so that potential clients can find you and easily learn more about your business with a click.

Choosing a Domain Name

Your domain name will be the web address of your business website. The Virtual Assistant Forums domain name is www.virtualassistantforums.com. That's what people type in and bookmark to visit the site directly. The domain name you choose for your own website should be easy to remember, not too long, and ideally it should reflect your chosen business name in some way, if not exactly. It is true that many of the premium domain names are already spoken for, and if you're not willing to pay the premium price to get the domain you want, you may need to compromise a bit on the domain you end up purchasing. For this reason, it's a good idea to brainstorm more than one possible domain name.

Once you've decided on the domain name(s) you want to purchase, you'll need to visit one of the online domain registration websites (search Google for "domain registration") to find out whether the domain is available, and purchase it if it is. Shop around a bit before you select a registrar; you can often find .com domain registration offers for as little as $5.00 per year. The average cost to register a domain for one year is $8.00 to $10.00.

Some registrars will allow you to register a domain for 2 years or more at a time, providing even more savings. Just be sure you're ready to commit to the domain for the long haul if you choose this option as fees for domain registration are rarely refundable even if you change your mind, change your business name, or decide to close your business altogether.

Once you've secured a domain name, the next step is to decide where you'll host your website.

Selecting Website Hosting

There are too many Web hosting companies (Google "website hosting") out there to count, and it can be difficult at first glance to narrow the options to the one that will best serve your goals and needs. Before making a choice, ask other VAs who they host with and what they like about the service they're using. Often your best options will come via referral. You can also use the following checklist to help you shop around to get the best deal, with the most features.

- **Uptime:** Obviously you want your site to be online 24/7, but the reality is, even the biggest, best-fortified sites go down from time to time. A good web hosting company has staff on-site 24 hours a day to handle any outages, technological issues, or crashes that will undoubtedly occur. An excellent Web hosting company boasts (and can prove) at least 99.5% uptime.

- **E-mail accounts:** One of the benefits of having your own domain is being able to use your own company e-mail addresses (Example: you@yourcompany.com). Incredibly, not all web hosts or hosting packages allow for this. Make sure you choose a hosting package that includes the ability to set up, manage, and use as many of your own e-mail addresses as you need. Also check for e-mail features like autoresponders and forwarding options.

- **Technical support:** It's important to think about your own communication style and needs in regards to customer service and technical support. Do you like to be able to dial a phone number any time of day or night to get the help you need, or are you comfortable submitting help desk requests through an online form or ticketing system? Each web hosting company handles customer and technical support in its own way, so be sure to take this into account before making your selection.

- **Customer satisfaction:** Taking the time to read online reviews from other business owners and customers of the web hosts you're considering can also help you in making the final decision.

Note that while there are numerous free hosting options available, this isn't necessarily the smart choice to make for your business. It can be tempting to go for a free hosting package, especially when you're getting your business off the ground and have a limited budget, but you should be aware of the relative limitations of using a free hosting service.

You do get what you pay for, and "free" often means little or no access to technical support should something go wrong, as well as extremely limited software for creating and updating your website. If you are going to host your site with a free web host, be sure to look for reviews from other users to get a better understanding of what you are (and aren't) getting.

Regardless which website hosting company you select for your site initially, know that it doesn't have to be a lifetime commitment. Most hosting companies charge on a monthly basis, so if you find a better hosting package with another company later on, you can always make a switch. Just be sure you're aware of your current hosting company's cancellation policies and that you have all of your website files backed up before you cancel at your current host.

Creating Your Website: Content

Now that have your domain and web hosting set up, the next step is to create a website for and about your virtual assistant business.

Whether you have your site professionally built for you (this can cost anywhere from about $350 and up) or you choose to design it yourself, there is some basic content you should consider including.

- **"Home" page:** You have about ten seconds to get website visitors interested in what you have to offer and turn them into potential clients. Your home page should quickly sum up how you can solve the problems of your target market and invite them to click further into the site to read more and/or sign up to receive your newsletter/blog feed, etc. Capture their attention *and* their e-mail addresses (if you're building a list), and you're halfway to a full practice.

  Even if you don't have any intention of using your site to build a list of prospects, at the very least your home page should provide an overview of what you have to offer as a virtual assistant. The text on your home page should be bold enough to state your strengths and creative enough to draw in your clients.

- **"About" page:** Whether you call it "About us," "About XYZ Company," or something else, this page gives you the opportunity to explain why you're unique as a virtual assistant. What exactly do you offer that makes you special? What kind of skills, talents and background do you bring to the table? This page should answer the question "Why?" as in, Why should your prospective clients select *your* services over the hundreds, if not thousands, of virtual assistants on the 'net?

- **"Services" and/or "Rates" page(s):** Anyone considering hiring you should know what their financial commitment is going to be like. On this page, you delineate your services and what you're likely to charge for them. You can also include information about your invoicing practices and payment terms as well as detail any discounts or packages you have to offer.

- **"Press" page:** Use this page to showcase any news that's made it to the virtual network or print media. Whether you've submitted a press release yourself or your company has been honored with a mention in another article or blog, this is the place to share the news.

- **"Articles" and/or "Newsletters" page(s):** Give website visitors (and search engines) a reason to return to your site by sharing informative articles you've written and/or an archive of your e-mail newsletter. This is another great place to ask users to sign up for a subscription to your newsletter if you have one.

- **"FAQ" page:** The FAQ (Frequently Asked Questions) page is where you can answer all of your website visitors' questions about virtual assistance. Answer the what, when, why, where, and how in a way that will appeal to your target market.

- **"Contact" page:** Possibly the most important page on your site, the contact page should allow clients to quickly and easily get in touch with you to learn more and get additional questions answered. Providing a contact form is a good start, but don't make it too long or ask for too much information at this stage; make it easy for those potential clients to reach out to you. Consider providing a phone number, e-mail, and address or P.O. box. This is a great place to include links to your social media profiles as well.

- **Blog:** A blog is a cost-effective way to provide visitors to your website (those crucial potential clients) with engaging, informative content to get them interested in what you have to say, impress them with your expertise, and keep them coming back to your site. Having a blog on your website is also an excellent way to enhance the SEO value of your site. You'll find more information on the benefits of blogging and how to use a blog for your own business growth in the next chapter.

Standing Out from the Crowd

Consider just how many virtual assistants there are out there. In that context, creating a website that shines in professionalism, presentation, content, and aesthetics is all the more important. Standing out from the crowd with a truly well-done website is just one way of distinguishing yourself from the many VAs crowding the global marketplace. A professional site engages potential clients and inspires them to want to learn more about you. A site that projects a professional image of you and your business even adds credibility.

Website Dos and Don'ts

To ensure your site provides the professional online persona your clients are expecting, follow this short list of dos and don'ts when creating your own site.

DO...

- **Pay attention to spelling, grammar, and coherency when writing the content for your website.** Potential clients will not be impressed with a website full of typos and poor writing when looking for a VA.

- **Consider including a picture of yourself along with a short bio.** Studies* have shown that people react, respond and relate to images of the human face. Giving your website visitors something positive to relate to (your smiling face) naturally increases the chances of their remembering you/your site/your company name and being inclined to reach out to and trust you more readily.

*Theeuwes, Jan, and Van der Stigchel, Stefan. "Faces capture attention." Visual Cognition, Volume 13, Issue 6: April 2006, pages 657 – 66.

- **View your website in multiple browsers.** It would seem like you should be able to create your website and assume it will look the same and as you intended in every browser, but that's just not the case. Download at least the top few browsers and check your site for any inconsistencies, differences, or other issues. A site that's perfect when viewed in Chrome or Firefox may look broken in Internet Explorer. We recommend checking your site in Chrome, Firefox, IE (the two latest versions if possible), and Safari (Safari for Windows if you are not on a Mac). You can also use an online service like the free Browser Shots (http://browsershots .org/) to see what your site looks like in many different browsers.

DON'T…

- **Don't toss up a "good enough" website in a hurry.** What does it say to your potential clients about your commitment and follow-through if you leave things halfway done for your own business?

- **Don't automatically go for the "free" website option.** Think about how a free website service might reflect on your professionalism and commitment to your own business. If your website is plastered with the advertising or affiliate links so often used by free website companies to recoup costs, what impression your potential clients develop?

- **Don't use cheap-looking, poor quality design elements.** That includes animated graphics, music, advertisements, lengthy flash introductions, or anything else that's going to distract from a professional image and your own company's marketing message.

- **Don't publish poorly articulated content, or not enough/too much content.** If your pages are difficult to read and understand or are so long that visitors have to scroll down more than once to get the message, you're losing potential clients. Help your visitors get in, get the information they need to make a decision, and get in touch with you quickly and easily.

- **Don't copy information about virtual assistants from** Wikipedia **(or any other page, for that matter) onto your home page.** This shows zero creativity and can be construed as plagiarism. Besides, you need to be able to explain what you do in your own words.

- **Don't copy content from another virtual assistant's website.** This really should go without saying. Plagiarism is unprofessional, period. And if stolen content is reported to Google, it's enough to get a site removed from Google's index, rendering a website virtually useless. In some cases of content theft, a site can even be taken down from the web entirely by the hosting provider.

Get Some Link Love

Once your site is complete, it's time to start using it as the marketing tool that it is. The first step is to get it indexed by the various search engines and get it listed in the better virtual assistant directories online. This helps the clients who need your services—and even those who don't know they need you (yet)—find you more easily. Use the links provided below to quickly index your site with the major search engines.

- To submit your site to **Google:** http://www.google.com/addurl/?continue=/addurl

- To submit your site to **Bing**: http://www.bing.com/webmaster/SubmitSitePage.aspx

- To submit your site to the **Virtual Assistant Forums Directory**: http://www.virtualassistantforums.com/directory/

Be sure to include a link to your website in your various social networking profiles. Completing your forum profiles with full information about your services and a link back to your site is another way to help get your site indexed faster and bring in more traffic. And don't forget to keep the information on your site current and updated to keep the search engines coming back and increase your site's visibility on the net.

Visit the Your Virtual Assistant Business Website section of Virtual Assistant Forums to get your questions answered and find additional discussion on and resources for: Domain Registration and Hosting, Website Coding, Website Content, and more. There's even a section where you can submit your completed VA business website for review by your fellow virtual assistants! (http://www.virtualassistantforums.com)

SECTION SIXTEEN

Your Business Blog

A blog is a cost-effective way to provide visitors to your website (those crucial potential clients) with engaging content to get them interested in what you have to say, impress them with your expertise, and keep them coming back to your site. Having a blog on your website is also an excellent way to enhance the SEO value of your site.

Benefits of Blogging

SEO (Search Engine Optimization)

When your website is consistently updated with fresh content, you give the search engines more reason to index your site as well as more pages to return in relative searches. Having a blog on your virtual assistant business site is an excellent way to make that happen because each new blog post equals fresh content and a new page. Just make sure that you're writing for your human visitors first and foremost; too much attention to keywords can leave your content literally unreadable. And don't fill your blog with puff-pieces just for the sake of landing traffic; you'll ultimately turn off your target audience once they realize they've been duped into clicking through to a blog that doesn't provide useful information.

Establish yourself as an expert

Leverage the power of the written word through your blog by showcasing your knowledge, skills, and expertise. A well-written blog post can speak volumes to a potential client about your business philosophy, organizational skills, communication style, understanding of the complexities of your particular niche, and overall professionalism.

Interact to create more prospects

A blog is interactive by nature, with the ability for readers to leave comments on each blog post. Providing this conversational aspect on your site gives it a more personal touch, but it also gives you the chance to learn even more about your potential clients and target market in general if your blog posts can draw them into a conversation by inspiring a comment.

Make announcements

Use your blog to publicize company news and events. Your blog is a great place to brag a little. Post announcements when your company adds a new service, when you master a new skill or receive a new certification, or even when you take on a new client.

Choosing a Blogging Platform

To start blogging, you'll need to choose one of the many platforms (Google "blogging platform") out there. Some blog platforms are designed to be hosted on your own domain (http://www.yoursite.com/yourblog) while others are hosted at their parent site (http://www.someblogsite.com/yourblog). Ideally, you'll host the blog on your own site as this gives you more control and flexibility and is overall the more professional choice. It's also better in terms of SEO (Search Engine Optimization) because it puts the content directly on your own domain.

While there are certainly many good blogging platforms available, we recommend exploring WordPress (http://www.wordpress.org). WordPress is a popular free blogging platform that you can host on your own website as well as integrate with your website's design. Word-Press boasts an enormous following and therefore has an endless array of features, widgets, plugins, hacks, premade design templates, mods, and so on available to help you create, launch, and enhance your blog. The WordPress admin panel is also easy to navigate, easy to learn, and extremely flexible. Wordpress is an undisputed favorite in the blogging world. This platform is so feature-packed and so flexible, it is often used as a CMS (content management system) to create entire websites.

Using the instructions provided in the WordPress Codex (http://codex.wordpress.org/New To WordPress - Where to Start) you can install a WordPress blog on your website. Or, check with your hosting provider as many Web hosts now include automated software that will quickly install WordPress for you. There are also many virtual assistants who specialize in WordPress blogs and websites and can help you for a fee. However you ultimately go about getting the blog on your website, as a budding entrepreneur, it never hurts to at least give it a shot. Dig in and see what you can accomplish yourself. You just might surprise yourself and discover a new skill to practice. And if it doesn't turn out to be your cup of tea, at least you can say you tried.

If you do choose to install WordPress yourself, you'll need to be able to access and work with your website files via FTP (file transfer protocol). It's not as intimidating as it sounds. This is the software that will allow you to upload the WordPress files to your website, actually creating the blog pages on your domain. A reliable, open-source FTP software you can download free is FileZilla (http://filezilla-project.org/). FileZilla, like WordPress, also has great documentation and tutorials (http://wiki.filezilla-project.org/Documentation) to help you learn to use the software.

Top Blogging Platforms to Explore

- WordPress: http://www.wordpress.org
- Moveable Type: http://www.movabletype.org/
- TypePad: http://www.typepad.com/
- Serendipity: http://www.s9y.org/
- Posterous: https://posterous.com/
- Tumblr: http://www.tumblr.com/
- Square Space: http://www.squarespace.com/
- B2evolution: http://b2evolution.net/
- Expression Engine: http://www.expressionengine.com/

Getting Started

Once you've got the technical side of things worked out, you're ready to start blogging! The idea of starting and maintaining a blog is intimidating for many people, VAs or otherwise, but blogging doesn't have to be scary or feel like a burden.

Start slow. Don't expect yourself to blog every single day, and don't be too hard on yourself. At the beginning, plan to blog one to two times per week. Try to prepare numerous ideas and posts in outline form in advance so you have plenty of material to choose from going forward. If you don't believe yourself to be a writer, stick to reporting on new stories, events, and lists until you feel more comfortable in your ability to convey your intelligence and professionalism via your blog.

Top Ten Ideas for Blog Posts

1. **Identify at least one common problem or pain point** that your target market deals with. Use your blog post to provide solutions.

2. **Share your top 3-5 small business resources.** Explain how to use them and why your target market will find them useful.

3. **Share your opinion on a relevant, controversial, or recent news story.** Explain your thoughts and impressions.

4. **Answer business-related questions** you've received via e-mail or come across on forums or social media sites.

5. **Subscribe to Google News Alerts** using keywords related to your target market. Watch the headlines for important news stories to share.

6. **Interview a key figure in your target market**, and share the conversation as a blog post or a series of blog posts.

7. **Review a book, product, or service related to your target market.**

8. **Attend and report on an industry-related event or convention** (either online or live).

9. **Use lists.** Create blog posts around lists of top blogs, newsletters, websites, books, software, events, resources, etc., that would benefit your target market.

10. **Blog about what you know.** Your website only gives a snapshot of your expertise and experience. Write blog posts that allow you to highlight your knowledge and skills.

For even more information and further discussion with other virtual assistants on the benefits of blogging, the various blogging platforms (and plug-ins), free design themes, and even to generate topics for your own blog, visit the Blogging section at Virtual Assistant Forums (http://www.virtualassistantforums.com/blogging) (Pssst!.... Need a 'quiet' place to test your blogging skills before you take the plunge? There's a free, easy-to-use SEO-friendly blog attached to your profile at Virtual Assistant Forums – no download needed, just log in and get started! Take a look at what Virtual Assistant Forum members are blogging about this week in the VAF Community Blogs (http://www.virtualassistantforums.com/blogs/)

SECTION SEVENTEEN

How to Respond to Requests for Proposals (RFPs)

There are many ways to locate and contract with new clients, including responding to RFPs (requests for proposal). This is when potential clients detail a problem they need solved or a project they need completed, and invite professionals to pitch bids for their services and solutions. You'll find RFPs at virtual assistant forums, job boards, or freelance sites, or even sometimes in the potential client's blog or in a company newsletter.

Most of the RFPs you encounter as a virtual assistant are going to be relatively informal.

Formal proposals (usually required by large corporations) do follow a specific format and will often require a financial prospectus, project risk analysis, and more. If you find yourself needing to prepare a proposal of this nature, the advice given below applies as well. However you come across an RFP, and whether it comes from a fellow small business owner or a multi-billion dollar corporation, there are a few simple guidelines to follow to ensure your response receives the attention it deserves.

Follow Directions!

It's a skill you started learning in your earliest years, yet it cannot be stressed enough. An RFP is a request for a response to a specific problem, need, or issue. It will often include specific instructions for format, delivery, or presentation that must be followed if you expect to be taken seriously by the potential client.

For example, Company A submits an RFP to your favorite VA forum and it's a perfect match for your skills and talents. The RFP states that "all proposals should be sent via e-mail with the subject line <u>WordPress Virtual Assistant</u>." This might not seem like a big deal, but many virtual assistants will put themselves out of the running automatically by failing to follow such a simple request. Title your RFP with anything other than "WordPress Virtual Assistant," and it's guaranteed to go straight into the Deleted Items folder.

The same goes for requests to include a link to your portfolio (if applicable) or other work samples. If you're asked to provide writing samples, be sure to include them and in the number and manner the client requests. (Note: Always provide samples of work you have *already* produced. Never provide a fresh writing sample to a prospective client, no matter how tempting it may be. You'd essentially be giving away your work free in that case.)

Provide responses to *all* of Company A's questions and requests, but be brief; the company is looking to contract a VA, not read a novella.

If a potential client asks for your résumé, CV, or references, you may need to politely educate them with a brief note explaining that as a professional service provider, you no longer operate with a résumé, as employees do, but that you've happily provided them with your brochure (or similar) and a link to the testimonials on your website from existing clients. This does mean you run the risk of losing the account by not providing a résumé, but if Company A operates with its contractors from an employee-employer approach, it may not be your ideal client.

Flex Your Research Skills

Company A's RFP also explains a need for a WordPress expert to help with "updating the company website, SEO through regular blog posting, and possibly the addition of a plugin." You're well versed in all things WordPress, so you start drafting your reply to Company A—but wait. Read the rest of the RFP first. Who is this company? What does the company do, and how and why is it done? If Company A hasn't given insight into all of those questions in the body of the RFP, it's time to do some homework and find out for yourself. Use your research skills to learn at least the basics about the company before drafting your response. The more you understand the client's industry and mission, the better equipped you are to provide a truly relevant response to the RFP. And you'll be at an advantage when you get a surprise call from the client looking for more information about how your company can help.

Follow Up (Again!)

Persistence is sometimes what wins a new contract. Businesses are, well, busy. Oftentimes that busy-ness which is the very reason a company goes in search of virtual assistance is the same reason the company isn't able to see plans through to fruition—they're just too busy. However much potential clients may truly want to select and contract with a virtual assistant, they may not always be able to keep their own process of selection moving. Help with that: If you don't hear back from a company regarding your proposal, don't be shy about politely, professionally following up. Ask whether your information was received and inquire whether you can schedule a time to discuss the company's needs.

At worst, you'll be told the company has chosen another service provider or you are no longer in the running. If that's the case, you've lost nothing by asking. But what if that extra nudge your questions give is all it takes to get the client back on the task of choosing a VA? If you're the service provider who shows initiative and inspires the potential client to action, you're more likely to be the one to win the contract.

For more in-depth discussion with your fellow virtual assistants on how to determine which RFPs you should respond to, and how to send a professional response visit Virtual Assistant Forums (http://www.virtualassistantforums.com).

Also be sure to check out the latest RFPs submitted by real potential clients to VAF's free RFP system (Note: you'll need a minimum number of posts contributed to the community before you can access RFPs and get the client's contact details – this helps ensure only those members most invested in the VAF community have access to this premium FREE resource. But don't worry, with all the questions and answers, hello's, and resource sharing you'll be doing on the boards, you'll reach the minimum post count in no time!)

Sample RFP

Following is a sample RFP. Using the information you've just read, practice drafting your response to the potential client. Note that this sample RFP is not indicative of all RFPs. Many times you will have nothing more to go on than a vague idea of who the client is and what he or she wants.

Client Name: Mary Jones

Client E-mail: mary@maryjonescompany.com

Company Name: Green Business Consulting

Company Information: I help businesses "go green" and reduce the environmental impact they make in their community and globally.

Industry: Green Business and Environmental Impact Consulting

Job Title: Help with organization and online research

Job Description: I no longer have time to keep my schedules, paperwork, and e-mail organized. I need someone who can help me stay on top of things, make sure appointments are made and kept, e-mails are responded to and filed as necessary, and so on. I am expanding my client base to include larger firms and need a VA who is experienced in online research and can gather information about which corporations my services could benefit and why, in preparation for a marketing campaign aimed at potential clients in this sector. I also want to start a blog or a newsletter, update my website, and refresh some of my existing marketing materials.

Special Skills: My virtual assistant must be very organized with acute attention to detail. A good communicator. Excellent at tracking down information online quickly and recording it accurately. If you have experience in marketing this is great, but not required.

Proposal Submission Requirements: E-mail with subject line "Virtual Assistant" and tell me why you're the right VA for me and how you can help get me organized. Also include rate info and a link to your website with writing samples.

The Art of Getting Paid: Billing and Invoicing

No matter how successful you are at running your business and landing clients, if those clients don't pay their bills, you won't have a business to run. As much as you may sincerely like your clients, you are not in the business of extending credit – you are not a bank or a charity. You are in business to make a profit. Your clients will benefit from your hard work, and you should expect to be compensated for that work according to the terms you set forth. With that in mind, you'll want to put a few policies and procedures in place to circumvent issues of late or non-payment altogether.

Time and Task Tracking

In order to invoice your clients accurately, you'll need to establish a method for keeping track of the time you've spent on their projects. From research to conference calls to putting the finishing touches on the product itself, invoicing correctly means properly tracking the time involved with all of those activities and attributing them to the right client.

There are a number of resources, from online services to mobile applications and desktop software, available for this purpose. (Google "time and task tracking" for a listing.) Some are free, but most are paid. Free time tracking applications tend to be fairly basic, but if you don't need a lot of bells and whistles, they could suit your needs perfectly. If you're looking for the ability to send branded invoices, sign clients in to a project log, and more, you'll probably want to choose a more full-featured service for a fee.

Features of a good time tracking application

- **Accurately tracks time by task:** Obviously your application must have the ability to accurately track, to the minute, the time you spend working on a client's projects. Ideally though, the application will allow you to create individual tasks and break down your time accordingly.

- **Multiple client and project management:** A truly useful time tracking application will allow you to create entries for multiple clients and track time on multiple projects. As your company grows, you'll be working with a larger client base and juggling more projects of all sizes. Choose a time tracker that can grow to accommodate the needs of your company one or more years from now.

- **Downloadable time log:** If you plan to provide a report to your clients of how much time you spent on which projects, this feature will make it much easier. Even if you won't be routinely supplying this information on your invoices, it can be a helpful feature should a client question a particular charge or invoice.

- **Generates invoices:** The most full-featured time and task tracking software will do more than just help you track the hours you've spent. It'll also help you get paid for that time. Look for a time tracking application that allows for branded invoicing so that you can include your own logo and your company payment terms and policies.

As always, one of the best ways to narrow the many choices available is to seek the advice of your fellow virtual assistants. More established business owners can vouch for the usefulness, affordability, and range of features of their chosen time tracking program or method, so be sure to read conversations on the virtual assistant forums if you find it difficult to make a choice.

You'll find plenty of resources, software options, and tips and tricks for effective, efficient time tracking from your fellow VAs in the Project Management section of Virtual Assistant Forums (http://www.virtualassistantforums.com).

Billing for Your Time

There are essentially three methods of billing that work well for a virtual assistant business: retainer, hourly, and per-project. Some VAs offer a mix of these or even all three. Others prefer to operate on a retainer-only basis. The following information provides some important thinking points to help you decide which billing method will be right for you and your company.

Billing on Retainer

When billing clients on a retainer basis, you'll be collecting payment in advance, for a specific number of hours, usually applied to the forthcoming month. Retainers are often delivered in packages of hours per month—5 hours, 10 hours, or more—and are meant to be "spent" by the client in the month for which they are purchased. Some virtual assistants will create tiered pricing levels, favoring the purchase of larger packages with a discounted rate.

Retainer hours generally do not roll over to the next month if they are not used by the client although some virtual assistants handle unused hours differently. Retainers are also non-refundable as a general rule.

A working relationship based on retainer is usually contracted between the client and the VA for a specific period of time: 3 months, 6 months, etc. When you accept a retainer client at a specific number of hours per month, you must ensure you will be available to handle the client's requests for the full amount of those hours, during the entire retainer period.

Billing on retainer can be beneficial because it offers

- **Predictable income:** Retainer billing allows you to be certain, in advance, of how much income you will earn each month.

- **Predictable workload:** Being on retainer also means easier time management as you'll generally know how much time each client will require each month.

Billing by the Hour

If you adopt the pay-as-you-go concept, you'll be charging your client on a per-hour basis only as and when the work comes in.

Billing by the hour offers the following advantages:

- **Simplicity:** Pay-as-you-go billing is simple as you only charge clients for the hours that you've worked, usually after the fact. There is no concern about "unused" hours, or having to be available for a specified time each month, for an extended period of time.

- **Easier for new clients:** New clients who don't yet know how much work they will require of you, or aren't ready to commit to a long-term contract right away, may be more comfortable with billing by the hour. You can always implement a different billing policy at a later date if it suits you and your client to do so.

Billing by the Project

If you'll be working on very large or highly technical projects such as web development or database design, you may wish to bill by the project. Billing by the project means creating an estimate or a quote for your client's approval. If you offer an estimate, you leave the project open to incremental billing based on the actual amount of work that it takes to complete. Estimates should always be as accurate as possible for obvious reasons. If you offer your client a quote you are placing a final price on the project, leaving no question for your client how much the work will cost, regardless of how long it takes.

Most virtual assistants who bill per-project will require an advance deposit of 25-50% of the estimate or quote before work begins. Deposits are generally not refundable, but again, different service providers utilize the approach and policy that works best and feels right for them.

Invoicing

Whether you bill hourly, on retainer, or per-project, or employ a mix of all three, in order to get paid for the work that you have done, or are going to do, you'll need to send your client an invoice, or a bill.

Your invoice should be presented in the same professional manner as all other business paperwork. It should be organized and easy to read and understand.

Each virtual assistant has a unique way of invoicing, but there are a few traits common to a good invoice template. Invoices should include:

- your business name, address, and other contact details
- your client's business name and address
- the date of the bill
- the due date
- a breakdown of the charges
- hourly rate, project fees, or retainer package rate
- hours worked or the blocks of time utilized
- discounts or credits applied
- penalties or late fees applied
- charges for incidental expenses
- taxes, if any
- the total amount due
- your payment terms and late payment policies.

You may also wish to consider including your company logo and tagline, an invoice number or account number (if applicable), and a log of work performed.

> Use the Invoice Template provided at the back of the book
> as a model to create your own branded invoice.

Visit the Rates and Billing section at Virtual Assistant Forums (http://www.virtualassistant forums.com/rates-billing) to ask questions, share and discover resources, and learn more about billing and invoicing options.

Payment Terms

Ideally, you've included your payment terms in your contract so that all clients are fully aware, from the start, of what their responsibilities are when it comes to reconciling invoices. Stipulate clearly how often you invoice, when invoices are due, and which methods of payment you accept. You may also wish to include the same payment terms on every invoice, completely avoiding any question or potential misunderstanding regarding your policies.

Depending on your own preference, you may choose to invoice your clients monthly, bi-monthly, or when a project is completed. You may require a deposit up front with the balance due upon completion of a specific project. If you're operating on a retainer, you'll want to stipulate when advance payments must be received and any penalties for a late or lapsed payment. If you choose to work on an hourly or per-project basis, the payment terms you develop and implement should ensure that you get paid frequently enough to maintain adequate cash flow in your business while also being sensitive to the fact that pay-as-you-go clients need a reasonable amount of time to pay the balance due.

Make it easy for your clients to pay you by offering as many payment methods as you are able. Some virtual assistants only accept payments via PayPal (http://www.paypal.com), Intuit Payment Network (https://paymentnetwork.intuit.com/), or similar online invoicing and payment systems. Others accept checks by post or direct deposit to their business bank account. Choose the payment method or methods that work best for you and your clients.

Handling Late Payments

Regardless how much effort you put into your invoicing methods and payment policies, you will almost certainly eventually have to deal with a late paying client. If your payment policies are complete and include penalties for lapsed payments, implementing the penalties according to your policies will simply be a matter of course.

A single late payment isn't the end of the world, and it doesn't have to mean the end of a good client relationship. If you have well-defined policies in place, you can impose a late payment penalty without feeling guilty about it, treating the penalty as the matter of course that it is, with the expectation that your client, having fully understood and agreed to your policies, will do the same.

Habitual late payments, on the other hand, can be the beginning of the end for your business. Without reliable cash flow, you simply cannot afford to remain in business, and you'll be wasting valuable time chasing down payments for work you've already done. Clearly defining the consequences of late payments, and imposing those consequences without fail, will help potentially late-paying clients take the due date on your invoices seriously.

There may be times when your client has a cash flow problem and communicates with you early and honestly about when you can expect payment. It's up to you to decide how to handle this scenario. If it's a long-term client who has always been consistent in making timely payments, you may wish to extend a little courtesy and be flexible in this particular instance. If it's a new client or a habitually late-paying client, you should be more cautious. You don't want to set a precedent of allowing late payments, especially with a new client. In these cases, you would be wise to apply any late payment penalties immediately.

> Copy and edit the Informal Late Payment Letter and/or
> the First Late Payment Collection Letter provided at the
> back of the book to include your own company's
> late payment policies, logo, tagline, contact information, etc.
> should you need to follow up on a late invoice.

Keeping Clients Means Keeping Clients Happy

As a business owner and service provider, you'll constantly be working to impress and connect with potential clients, but don't forget to place the same emphasis (if not more) on your relationships with existing clients. These are the clients who are literally keeping you in business and will be the first to refer their friends and colleagues to you. Honoring that connection and keeping the relationship strong leads to long-term loyalty and a stronger bottom line for your company. Whether you have one client or ten, you're going to want to do what you can to ensure that your business relationships with them continue to grow, develop, and deepen.

Long-Term Client Relations

Be One Step Ahead

Every client wants to feel like they are your most important client, or even your only client. Of course they know that's not the case, but in your clients' perfect world, you are available to them anytime they need you, without fail. You're their go-to, their problem solver, their life saver. Without sacrificing your own business policies and boundaries, embrace the role and do what you can to make life easier for them. Your keen sense of anticipation of their needs can go a long way to impress in a business relationship. Act proactively in your client's favor, and you'll become truly indispensible.

Ask Questions

Never underestimate the power of a simple e-mail or phone call, especially if you have lingering questions about the project you've been tasked with. By sending a quick request for clarification as soon as you realize more information is necessary, you'll avoid misunder-standings, wasted time, and disappointed clients. Whether you're on a tight deadline or have weeks to completion, take the time to ask your questions as soon as they crop up. Your client will appreciate your thoroughness, and the project you deliver will be completed correctly.

Communicate

Always keep your clients up-to-date on a project or situation at hand, even if it's just a brief e-mail. Nothing feels more precarious for a client working virtually than to send you a project and not hear anything in return. Let your clients know when you receive their requests, keep them updated on when you can get started, and touch base at various points throughout the course of the project so they know how things are progressing and can address questions or changes as they arise. If you're unable to complete a project on time, let them know. If you run into unplanned issues, let them know about it and offer solutions. Lack of communication is deadly for a business relationship. Consistent, clear communication keeps things moving and gives the relationship stability, which leads to longevity.

Do What You Say You Will, When You Say You Will

Reliability is a learned trait for some but should be an innate characteristic for a virtual assistant. If you tell a client you're going to make that deadline, schedule those calls, file the paperwork, submit their proposal, etc., you'd better be prepared to get it done—and done on time. When your clients know they can rely on you, they can relax a little more. Imagine how invaluable that makes you.

Quality Check

Don't let the quality of your work slide, even just a little. Ever. There will come a time when you realize you no longer have to work so hard to impress your client, but don't take for granted the importance of leaving them impressed over the long haul. A typo here, a missed memo there—it all adds up, and for some clients, those typos and memos can be very expensive mistakes. Of course, nobody is perfect and mistakes do happen. But by being totally present in the work in front of you, staying focused, and being attentive to immediate objectives, you'll minimize mistakes and spare yourself (and your client) the question of whether it's time to shop around for a new VA.

Reach Out

Once you build trust with your clients, you'll find that most interactions, projects, and transactions will go very smoothly. However, there may be times when you and your client don't see eye to eye on how a project should play out, or a misunderstanding occurs that causes tension in the business relationship. When something happens that causes a rift in what was before a wonderful working relationship, take the initiative and reach out to your client to see what can be done to repair any damage. If you've made a mistake or otherwise let your client down, be the first to admit it and the first to apologize. Your honesty will disarm your client and help temper any negative feelings. By seeking to find a solution to the problem early on, you avoid letting a bad impression fester. When the circumstance calls for deeper communication, e-mail simply won't do. Reach out to your client with an invitation for a phone call so you can efficiently work out any differences or misunderstandings.

Saying "Thank You"

After you and your clients have worked together for an extended period of time, be sure to let them know how much you appreciate their business and their loyalty to your company. Sending "thank yous" and/or small gifts commemorating the anniversary of the start of your relationship, upon contracting a new referral, or after the close of a big project is a wonderful way to let your clients know how important they are to you and your business. While it can be tempting to shoot off an e-mail expressing your sentiments, nothing gives the same impression as a handwritten card.

Here are just a few affordable client gift ideas:

- Make **a small donation** in your client's name to a cause you know they care about.
- Purchase **a gift certificate** for your client to a micro-lending site such as http://www.Kiva.org.
- Send **a home-baked gourmet treat** such as cookies or brownies.
- E-mail a gift certificate for **an hour or two of one of your services** or for a discount on their next invoice.
- Purchase **a gift certificate** for your client to a well-reviewed eatery or café in their neighborhood.
- Gift a new copy of **your favorite business or marketing book** to your client.
- Send your client **a magazine subscription** you know they will appreciate.

Asking for Feedback

It's important to touch base with your clients to ask for their feedback, but not too often; once or twice a year should suffice. Ask your clients specific questions related to their experiences working with you, and you'll get a good perspective on where you can improve, how you can better serve your clients, and ways in which you can grow your business.

Create a list of questions specific to your client base and send them out via e-mail, set up a survey on a site like Survey Monkey (http://www.surveymonkey.com) or Poll Daddy (http://www.polldaddy.com), or direct your clients to a URL on your own website where they can answer your questions.

Don't forget that your clients are busy, so don't ask too many questions at a time and try not to ask questions that require an essay to answer. If you want to provide some special incentive for client participation, consider offering a 10% discount on their next invoice or similar.

Use any of the questions below as you see fit to gather feedback and testimonials from your clients. Edit the questions to suit your own company language, directives, and services. Of course you can write your own questions as well. Remember that if you are going to quote any of your clients' responses as well as use their name and/or company name in your marketing materials or on your website, you should ask their permission first.

- Do you feel that we are readily available when you need us?
- Are there any services you wish we offered?
- Do you feel that your invoices and billing terms are fair and accurate?
- Are your requests handled in a timely and professional manner?
- How has my team been performing for you?
- How would you rate our overall level of service?
- Where do you feel we could improve our level of service?
- Would you say it was fairly easy to work with us?
- What would make it easier?
- What would make you say "WOW!"
- Are you happy with the service you've received?
- Has anything caused frustration or difficulty for you?
- How do you think we could have avoided it?
- Do you feel we communicate with you often enough?
- How can we help improve communication?
- Do you feel we listen and understand your requests, needs and concerns?
- In what areas did we meet or exceed your expectations?
- Why did you choose us as your service provider?
- How do we compare to other service providers?

Want to get more in-depth on this topic? Join the conversations, or start a new one, with your fellow virtual assistants in the Virtual Assistant / Client Relations section of Virtual Assistant Forums (http://www.virtualassistantforums.com).

SECTION TWENTY
When Things Don't Work Out: How to Fire a Client

Business relationships, like any other type of relationship, can go sour. Sometimes things with a particular client don't work out as we had expected and it becomes clear that things must change. As a business owner and service provider, it's usually in your best interest to try to salvage the relationship by opening a discussion about whatever it is that's upsetting or disruptive to you. But what if the client has proven to be a toxic personality, or exhibits ethics strongly opposed to your own? What if your client has turned out to be extremely high-maintenance, to the point of being unreasonable? There may be situations when you simply don't wish to try to salvage the relationship but would rather remove the issue entirely, opening space in your schedule for a new, more ideal client. As hard as it might be to imagine or accept, there may be times when firing your client is the best decision you can make for yourself and the success of your business.

You Know It's Time to Fire Your Client When...

...it becomes impossible to continue with a contracted relationship comfortably and efficiently. There are many reasons you might decide to stop working with a client, including:

Everything is an emergency

The first time your client e-mails you with ALL CAPS and the subject line "URGENT!" you're quick to respond and help solve the problem. After all, he e-mailed you during business hours and you had a few minutes to spare. But soon, you see a pattern developing with this client and realize that nearly all of his requests are framed as emergencies—even when they're not. Your client continually insists you find space in your schedule RIGHT NOW to address his to-do list.

Remember, your client's failure to plan is not your responsibility. If your client's inability to wait for an open slot in your schedule to see his requests addressed is starting to interfere with your ability to get work done for other clients, you've got a problem that's only going to get worse unless you confront it head-on. If, even after discussing the issue with your client and reiterating how you operate, you find you're being asked to make too many exceptions to your otherwise perfectly acceptable scheduling and turnaround policies, it might be time to let the client go.

Conflicting values and questionable ethics

Imagine your client asks you to update her website but sends you to her competitor's site for the content. You might think she doesn't realize plagiarism applies to the 'net the same as other content, and you might steer her in another direction with some gentle education. But when you realize the same client has lied to one of her clients, or is cheating her customers, the real picture begins to take shape.

Sometimes your issues with a client will stem from the realization that you simply have vastly divergent values. This isn't always a deal-breaker, and the worst can sometimes be avoided with a diplomatic but straightforward "No, I don't feel comfortable doing that." Only you can decide whether a particular issue is important enough to break ties. But if a client exhibits shady, unethical, or illegal business practices, you're probably wise to distance yourself to protect the reputation of your own business.

Constant haggling over price

The first few invoices you sent your client were paid on time or well before the due date, but she wrote back each time, prior to making payment, to ask whether you would consider giving her a discount. You politely decline each time and explain that you don't generally offer discounts, as your rates are very competitive given your level of expertise. You don't blame her for wanting to save money, and she does send a lot of work your way, so you let it pass and assume that's going to be the end of requests for discounts. But the client then tries another tactic and starts replying to your invoices with questions about the validity of particular charges, or complaints about how long a project took you to complete.

If your client signs your contract knowing exactly how much you charge but always asks you to justify your rates after the fact, you may want to consider letting the client go.

Toxic attitude

You're not sure whether your client's e-mail detailing all the things he didn't like about the completed project you just sent him is intentionally sarcastic and rude, but you don't want to appear sensitive to criticism, and you don't want to mistake his offer of sincerely constructive feedback for a toxic attitude, so you give him the benefit of the doubt and move on. But it's a similar scenario the following week as your client shoots your proposed marketing approach right back at you with nothing but criticism for your ideas and an exasperated tone that tells you he doesn't value you, your opinion, or your expertise.

It's a rare breed, the client who literally sneers at your best efforts, or seems to want to undermine your confidence as a service provider, but such clients do exist. If your client talks down to you or is constantly negative, downright rude, or even verbally abusive, don't tolerate the treatment.

Late or unpaid invoices

The first time your client pays an invoice late, she e-mails you on the due date with a sincere apology: It just slipped her mind, she's so busy this week! She tells you she's going to get the check out to you right away. You're grateful for the communication and let it slide this time without charging a late fee. A month later, it's the same story, only this time you have to e-mail her, twice, to get a check in the mail a week after it's due. And when the check does finally arrive, the postmark reveals that your client didn't send it out the day she assured you she would, but five days after that.

If a client chronically pays invoices late, or makes insufficient payments that result in carrying an unpaid balance, with no apparent efforts to make good on the debt, it's time to put an end to the relationship. Late-paying clients are as much a liability to your business as non-paying clients when you calculate the amount of time you must invest in chasing down the money you've earned. Late payments happen, and some amount of flexibility on your part is gracious, as long as your client pays the relative late fees and doesn't make a habit of it. But the client who is truly cavalier about paying your bills is not an ideal client.

There are other possible reasons to fire a client. Ask any group of established virtual assistants to share their own stories of having to let clients go, and you'll get some pretty wide-ranging responses. However you reach the conclusion that your own client is nowhere near the ideal you want to be working with, you're the only one who can take action and make a change. You first need to decide whether you want to try another approach before taking the final step of dissolving the relationship.

Alternatives to Saying Goodbye

If you rely too heavily on the income from your questionable client; if the client holds real status in your target market and you see opportunity you're not ready to walk away from (yet); if you can't find it within yourself to be so blunt as to fire your client; or if you're just not ready to give up on the relationship, there are a few alternatives you can try.

- **Talk it out:** There's only so much clarifying and rehashing you can do, and some clients just won't take what you have to say to heart. But if firing them isn't an option, keep trying to communicate the issues with your difficult client and ask for solutions.

- **Charge (a lot) more:** That's right! Charge your rude or otherwise less-than-ideal client more for the privilege of being difficult. If your client walks away as a result, you've still solved your problem.

- **Get over it:** You should never have to accept intolerable working conditions, but if you can't bring yourself to fire your client, you don't really have a choice but to endure. Until you find a way to fully embrace all that being a business owner requires and are willing to act, you're going to have to get over it.

Letting Go

When you've come to the difficult conclusion that it's time to fire your client, of course you'll want to do so without harming your professional reputation. Even if you would never agree to do business with that particular client again, you still want to do what you can to avoid burning bridges and minimize possible negative feelings. This is particularly important if the defunct client knows or works with any of your other clients. The last thing you want is to give any client reason to complain about you to others.

Here are a few tips for ending the working relationship gracefully.

- **Be professional:** Approach the end of the relationship the same way you approached the beginning: with professionalism. There is no room for emotion, blaming, or back-and-forth in this equation as it'll only serve to make what you have to do more difficult and complicated. Keep communications brief but friendly, to-the-point and void of blame, regret, or accusations.

- **Refer to your contract:** Your contract should have sufficient clauses to cover the eventuality of either party terminating the contract. Be sure to follow the exit strategy outlined in your contract to the letter. Return any deposits or apply them against your client's balance due. If your contract requires you to give your client notice, do it. Note that in cases of non-payment, you are not beholden to your client for the notice period and should NOT continue work for them under any circumstances. If there are outstanding projects you've already been paid for, wrap them up or negotiate with your client to end the project or pass it on to someone else. Once you've been paid for all services rendered, be sure to forward to your client any information you maintain on their behalf such as website passwords and access points, etc. Wrapping up all lose ends before you part ways will spare you from having to revisit an uncomfortable situation.

- **Offer alternatives:** If your issues with the client are personal rather than a discovery of illicit behavior, you might want to refer your client to one or two other possible replacements. But if you can't pass your client on to another service provider in good conscience, don't.

Firing a client can be one of the most stressful events in an entrepreneur's life, but you can and will get through it. Relief and empowerment replace the dread you felt every time you saw your client's name in your e-mail inbox. Realize that in closing one door, you open new windows of possibility for your business. The countless hours spent dealing with a less-than-ideal client can now be spent bringing in more business from your other clients as well as those very promising potential clients who will pay your invoices on time and treat you with the respect you deserve.

> Use the <u>Mutual Release from Contract</u>
> provided at the back of the book in situations
> where you want to officially sever all ties
> and contractual obligations with a difficult client.

There's an empathetic, supportive community of virtual assistants at VAF. Many have personal experience with the kinds of difficult scenarios described in this chapter. Visit the <u>Client Relations Issues</u> section of Virtual Assistant Forums for a private (not indexed by search engines, not visible to non-members) place to share your own stories, ask questions, and share advice with other VAs in similar situations. (<u>http://www.virtualassistantforums.com</u>)

SECTION TWENTY-ONE
New Skills = New Services

You're likely entering into your new virtual assistant business with a cache of marketable skills. Whatever your background experience and expertise, you've probably already given some thought to which services you will offer, how much you can charge for those services, and who you'll market them to. While it can feel great to have this knowledge in place as you prepare to launch your business, don't let yourself be content to the point of complacency.

As a virtual assistant, you're expected to have the most up-to-date understanding and working knowledge of new technologies and resources relative to your niche or specialty (and then some).

For example, if you set yourself up as a social media VA, your clients will assume you're not only a master at Twitter, Facebook, and LinkedIn but are also keeping abreast of, and ready to support the use of, all the additional sites and applications cropping up. You'll need to be aware of the latest trends making waves in the social media industry, knowing which ones are worth investing time and energy in and which are best left ignored. From managing social media more efficiently with HootSuite (http://www.hootsuite.com), to getting your client's company active on YouTube (http://www.youtube.com), to Stumbling (http://www.stumbleupon.com) your client's articles, to encouraging your client to use Foursquare (http://www.foursquare.com) for keeping track of (and mastering) the ever-changing landscape of social media marketing will be your responsibility while your clients focus on other aspects of business growth.

Or, another example: If you are marketing yourself as a virtual author's assistant, it's going to be important to have a working knowledge of the print publishing industry as well as the ever-growing options for digital and self-publishing. Knowing where to get an ISBN, how to submit a written work to the Library of Congress, and how to apply for copyright protection are just a handful of the assumed skills for someone in your niche. From legalities to book launches and marketing, it's all requisite knowledge. And with the publishing industry changing fast as metadata, ePubs, digital readers and print-on-demand take on larger roles, it will be your responsibility to not only be aware of changes, trends, and developments but be able to navigate them all on your client's behalf.

However you position yourself in the virtual assistance industry, whether your skills are highly technical or more administrative, you will eventually need to learn a new skill, a new application, or an entirely new way of doing something in order to keep up with your clients' increasingly sophisticated needs. If you don't keep up, your clients will ultimately outgrow your services.

In order to ensure you remain highly operational relative to trends and new information, it's necessary to seek out learning opportunities and dive in before your client approaches with a request you should know how to respond to, but don't.

Staying Ahead of the Curve

You can't be in a leadership position in your niche or industry unless you stay ahead of the curve. Take the social media virtual assistant mentioned earlier. If she (or he) learns of a new social media site or relative software application, she's going to schedule time to investigate it. She will register at the site or download the app to explore firsthand. By learning what she can about the resource's purpose and how it works, she can determine whether it might be an appropriate avenue for her clients to pursue. When she presents this new option to her clients and recommends they get on board, she not only backs up her status as a leader in her industry, she keeps her clients on the cutting edge of social media marketing—and creates more billable hours for herself in the process.

Getting Outside Your Comfort Zone

The opportunity for and importance of ongoing learning isn't limited to a virtual assistant's current niche or existing range of services. While it is necessary to keep existing services fresh and relevant, it's equally important to stretch outside that zone and incorporate skills that could result in an entirely new range of services. By continuing to develop new skill sets, a virtual assistant increases the number of needs that can be met, offering clients what they need and want, sometimes before they even realize they need or want it.

Jack of All Trades, Master of None

Be careful in your pursuit of new skills not to dilute the potency of what you already excel at. Sometimes it makes the most sense to invest in upgrading your knowledge of your current craft or adding only closely related services. Unless you're prepared to master a new direction, don't waste your time, energy and resources. Better to be a service provider with a concise service menu, with an end product delivered at 110% every time, than one with a long list of services provided at a mediocre level of quality. There's a lesson for all of us in the old saying "Jack of all trades, master of none."

SECTION TWENTY-TWO
The Good News and the Bad News

If you've read every chapter and worked through every exercise in this book, you're well on your way to launching your virtual assistant business.

> **The good news is**, the success of your virtual assistant business is totally up to you.
>
> **The bad news is**, the success of your virtual assistant businessis totally up to you.

It's Your Call

No one is going to pretend that what you're doing is easy or that it's going to get easier anytime soon—and neither should you. Building ANY business from the ground up is hard work, and a virtual assistance business is certainly no exception. If, after reading this book, you still think you're going to be able to print up a few business cards, launch a quick website, and sit back while the clients and the cash roll in, you're in for a rude awakening.

If you can do the work it takes to make a success of your own business, then you probably have what it takes to support other peoples' businesses. And that's what a virtual assistant does: provide ongoing administrative and specialized support to entrepreneurs and small business owners, virtually.

You really are the only one who can make that happen, or not. No one else can do it for you and there are no short cuts. The information in this book can help steer you in the right direction and give you a solid foundation to start from, but they're your goals. It's your business: Claim it. Commit to it. Make it happen. You can do it!

No Virtual Assistant Is an Island

As much as you are solely responsible for the outcome of your new business venture, it's not necessary to go it alone. Create a network of support starting with like-minded business people, especially other VAs.

There are numerous virtual assistant networks for you to join, both online and off. Whether it's a free membership at Virtual Assistant Forums (http://www.virtualassistantforums.com) or a local community group for small business owners, you'll find the support and encouragement you need to get through the tough times by investing in the networks that are a good fit for you. Many of these groups also have plenty of information to help you grow your business from the ground up and keep it growing after the startup phase. Virtual Assistant Forums is a great place to start, and the information provided at the site will complement all that you've learned by reading this book.

Sharing your plans with supportive friends and family members is another way to further build your network. The more cheerleaders you have on your sidelines, the more likely you are to succeed, so don't be shy about sharing your exciting business goals with those you trust to offer support and encouragement!

Taking Care of #1

Don't forget to be supportive of *yourself*. After all, you ARE your business. If you let yourself get burned out or succumb to negative thinking, you're not doing yourself or your (potential) clients any good.

It can be easy to feel overwhelmed by all that has to be done before you're officially in business. But if you take each step one at a time and don't rush through what's before you, you'll be able to pat yourself on the back for your great accomplishments.

Complete each part of the startup process with focus and determination and don't be too hard on yourself when it doesn't happen overnight, especially if you're also juggling a full- or part-time job outside the home, school, family, or more.

**With patience, focus, and dedication, you'll soon be able
to call yourself a Professional Virtual Assistant <u>with confidence</u>!**

A Day in the Life of a Virtual Assistant

by Janine Gregor, Your Virtual Wizard

(http://www.yourvirtualwizard.com)

Used with permission

I start out my day, waking with an alarm,
some mornings, that's tough,
as my covers are warm.

Husband has made coffee, pour the cream in my cup.
Wake up my teen. "Hey, you'd better stay up!"
Throw on my sweats, brush my teeth, wash my face,

Feed the cat, feed the teen, "Yes, it's oatmeal for darn sakes."
"Leave the iPod at home, don't even ask.
And please don't forget your books and school lunch pass."
(Help me this day, as I ignore his morning sass!)

We'd better get going;
I've got much on my plate; e-mails, Twitter,
social networking won't wait.

Already my head is a-spin;
I may be going berserk,
but I can't sit down 'til I finish my mom-work.

A quick drive to school, "Good luck on your test!"
A kiss and a hug, "And, please do your best."

He turns with a grunt then pauses to say,
"I love you too, Mom but please go away.
My friends are all looking, you see,
so please go to work, you're embarrassing me!"

The drive back home, I'm thinking of work;
a new client today, perhaps a contract to sign,
This is a great job, with so many fun perks.

I take off my taxi-cap and up to my door,
smile to the neighbor,
(oh that man's an incredible bore!)
Pick a few weeds, in the box goes the Netflix,
I've arrived right on-time,
oh, this office is a mess!

Phone conference at 10, computer goes on;
I must prepare.
Toss in some laundry, oops, that sweater's mohair.

Heat up the first coffee now cold from before;
only one cup remaining, shall I make some more?

Click on my Inbox, checked only 12-hours-past.
E-mails pour in like a flood,
I'd say, 20 mbps is rather fast.

Check boxes for client-rush requests,
check VAF for new posts,
comment LinkedIn, post Twitter
I'm working hard to deliver.

Look at my calendar, I've got real estate work,
new listings are posted with virtual tours to stitch.
I'll have to redo my weekly to-do list.

A client has e-mailed me she wants something fast...a newsletter copy;
she can't know I'm behind.
I'll open the attachment...what will I find?

Newsletter copy that needs more than a tweak,
bad spelling and formatting,
it does look rather bleak.

I get started on this rush project, in comes new real estate listings.
Get these up on the 'net, the agent is insisting.

Time moves quickly and I've completed all three tasks.
Sent off that newsletter, will the client approve fast?
Now I'm writing a blog post and stitching photos again,
I have to push hard, client conference awaits
and it's already 10.

Break away from my work to make my call,
new client is pleasant and seems rather fine.
Will he sign my contract and do so on-time?

Yes, I can update your ads and post listings to your sites,
write your blogs, articles and newsletters;
and make them look right.
Yes, I can help you for as long as you like, but remember,
your budget is really quite tight.

My day continues, finishing work as it comes in.
The newsletter copy is returned no changes…great, it's a win!

New client sent contracts, we'll get started the next day.
Set up new folders, passwords and names.

(This is a real business and I don't play games.)

I'm learning new programs, have QuickBooks Pro in the wings,
I'll be loading new software and reading manuals and such things.

The blog is nearly finished. I'll post to Active Rain.
What will be the next topic?

(Occasionally, I do think I am going insane.)

I finally step outside for some much-needed fresh air.
The blue Florida sky, the graceful palms and the birds.
How proud that this is my office; my life in my own words.

Time to pick up the teen, "Lord; give me strength if you may."
Surprisingly he asks me, "Mom, how was your day?"

He doesn't like his teacher; he wants to play with the Wii.
"Mom, I'll make you a deal. I'll do my homework for a fee."

I don't change diapers or take care of new babies, you see,
but I remain a VA as my teen still needs me.

Peer pressure, girls, homework and school,
he still needs a mom to listen each day;
albeit I'll agree, I am really 'uncool'.

My VA job allows me to choose,
the work that I like to do,
I contract with quality people
More or less, or perhaps just a few.

The best part of all, is that I can
be a Mom too.

Virtual Assistant
and
Small Business
Resources

Virtual Assistant Industry Resources

Virtual Assistant Forums Virtual assistants at all levels of business development network at Virtual Assistant Forums. This popular online community for VAs offers free virtual assistant resources and information. http://www.virtualassistantforums.com

Virtual Assistantville This premium virtual assistant directory features multi-page directory listings, giving you space to highlight more than just your services and a link to your website. Add a video, include your latest blog posts, share client testimonials and more! Four levels of membership starting at just $2.99 a month. http://www.virtualassistantville.com/

Virtual Assistant Forums Directory Virtual assistant directory listing VA businesses by location and specialty. Premium featured listings provide increased exposure for a small monthly fee. http://www.virtualassistantforums.com/directory/

Virtual Assistant Rate Comparison Calculator Customizable rate comparison calculator widget for use on your website and blog. Help potential clients understand the cost of working with a virtual assistant with this interactive calculator. Customize to your own site colors, company name, rate and contact information. http://www.virtualassistantforums.com/get_calculator.php

Start a Virtual Assistant Business Growing collection of articles and blog posts on the topic of starting a virtual assistant business. Also highlights various industry resources. Written by virtual assistants for virtual assistants. Read and comment on articles or submit your own work for publication. http://www.startavirtualassistantbusiness.com/

Virtual Assistant Information Blog dedicated to evangelizing the virtual assistant profession and educating the clients and potential clients of virtual assistants on how to find, contract, and work with a professional VA. http://www.virtualassistantinformation.com/

Create a Professional New Client Welcome Packet A Virtual Assistant Forums Guide. This 26 page, step-by-step, PDF how-to guide explains exactly what you must include in a welcome packet, then walks you through creating your own professional new client welcome packet. The guide also includes seven editable templates you can customize and use to create your new client welcome packet! (New Client Welcome Letter, New Client Intake Form, New Client Questionnaire, Credit Card Authorization Form, *ADDED BONUS* Comprehensive Retainer Contract) http://www.virtualassistantforums.com/store/

Office Applications

<u>Open Office</u> Open source software suite for word processing, spreadsheets, presentations, graphics, databases and more. http://www.openoffice.org/

<u>Libre Office</u> Free open source personal productivity suite for Windows, Macintosh and Linux, that gives you six feature-rich applications for all your document production and data processing needs: Writer, Calc, Impress, Draw, Math and Base. http://www.libreoffice.org/

<u>ThinkFree</u> Comprehensive online and mobile office applications. Word processing, spreadsheet and presentation functionality. http://product.thinkfree.com/

<u>Microsoft Office Professional</u> The Microsoft Office Suite includes Word, Excel, Access, Powerpoint, OneNote, Outlook, Office Web Apps and more. A full-featured office application collection Office is one of the most commonly used tools by virtual assistants. http://office.microsoft.com/en-us/business/

<u>ZOHO</u> A wide range of online applications. Zoho Business is an application and "platform" that combines a number of Zoho applications into a single dashboard where you can view and access all your documents. It also provides a sharable calendar, supports groups, contacts, e-mail, tasks and a means to add and pay for additional Zoho services. http://www.zoho.com/

<u>Google Docs</u> Create and share your work online and access your documents from anywhere. Manage documents, spreadsheets, presentations, surveys, and more all in one place. Supports real-time collaboration. docs.google.com/

<u>Adobe PDF</u> Convert and combine PDF files online. Free trial available. http://createpdf.adobe.com/

<u>PDF 995</u> Easily create professional-quality PDF documents with the click of a button. http://www.pdf995.com/

<u>Google Apps</u> Hosted communication and collaboration tools for any size. Google Apps includes Gmail for business, Google Docs, Google Calendar, Google Sites, and more. Yearly subscription fee. http://www.google.com/apps/intl/en/business/index.html

Multimedia Resources

<u>Jing Project</u> Take a picture or make a short video of what you see on your computer monitor. Share it instantly via web, email, IM, Twitter or your blog. Enhance online conversations and improve client communications. Offers a free and pro version. http://www.techsmith.com/jing.html

<u>Camtasia</u> Screen recording and video editing software. Turn screen recordings into polished video. Capture full screen, window or region. Add in music tracks, microphone, your computer's audio, plus picture-in-picture with your video camera. Powerpoint plugin available. http://www.techsmith.com/camtasia

<u>Audio Jungle</u> Selection of royalty-free stock audio, sound effects, and music for use in podcasts, online radio shows, websites, webcasts, etc. http://audiojungle.net/?ref=Codehead

<u>Vsnap</u> Vsnap makes it easy to send short video messages as a more personal alternative to email. A vsnap is 60 seconds, maximum. There's nothing to download. All you need are an internet connection and a camera on your computer, smartphone or tablet. Add attachments and send your Vsnap to any email address or directly to your Twitter feed. https://www.vsnap.com/

<u>Audacity</u> Audacity is free, multi-lingual, open source software for recording and editing sounds. use Audacity to: record live audio, convert tapes and records into digital recordings or CDs, edit Ogg Vorbis, MP3, WAV or AIFF sound files, cut, copy, splice or mix sounds together, change the speed or pitch of a recording, and more. http://audacity.sourceforge.net/

<u>YouTube</u> Discover, watch and share originally-created videos. Create a YouTube channel for your virtual assistant business and upload videos to share your video message with colleagues, clients, and potential clients. Provides embed code for adding your videos to your website or blog. http://www.youtube.com/

<u>Screencast</u> Solution for businesses looking to manage and share videos, images, documents, or anything else online. High-quality content-hosting gives you complete control over how, when and to whom your content is distributed. Free account up to 2GB. http://www.screencast.com/

<u>Ustream</u> Live interactive online broadcasting platform. Anyone with an internet connection and a camera can start engaging with viewers anytime, anywhere. Start your own channel to create and stream your own content. http://www.ustream.tv/

BlogTalk Radio Social Radio Network that allows anyone, anywhere the ability to host a live, internet talk radio show, simply by using a telephone and a computer. Integrated with Facebook, Twitter, and Ning. Start your own station to create and broadcast your own content. http://www.blogtalkradio.com/

Vimeo Video sharing site created and run by a community of filmmakers and video creators . Provides embed code for including videos on your own website and blog. Create a Vimeo account for your virtual assistant business and upload videos to share your video message with colleagues, clients, and potential clients. http://vimeo.com/

Tiki Toki Create interactive timelines that include videos and image galleries. Integrates with Flickr, YouTube and Vimeo. http://tiki-toki.com/

Slideshare Online presentation sharing community. Also supports sharing of documents, PDFs, videos and webinars. http://www.slideshare.net/

Prezi Cloud-based presentation software with interactive, zoomable canvas allows you to create visually captivating presentations. http://prezi.com/

Time Tracking, Invoicing and Scheduling Resources

Quickbooks Full-featured Small Business accounting and payroll software. Organize financial tasks, get an overview of your company finances, send invoices, make payments, track expenses, and more. Offers a free trial version. http://quickbooks.intuit.com/

Intuit Payment Network Send and receive payments online with a small business account for a flat per-transaction fee of just 50 cents. No monthly fees. Accept credit card payments. https://paymentnetwork.intuit.com/

PayPal Send and receive payments online with various account levels including business and ecommerce for a variable percentage fee plus a small per-transaction fee. No monthly fees. Accept credit card payments. Full-featured merchant services, payment gateways, IPNs and more. Allows for subscription invoicing. https://www.paypal.com

Square Accept credit card payments with your iPhone, iPad or Android phone. Download the free Square app to get started. Visit the website to order the free Square credit card reader for your mobile device. https://squareup.com/

My Intervals Web-based time tracking, task management, and project management for small businesses that need to know where all of their time is going. http://www.myintervals.com

Freshbooks Online time tracking, billing and invoicing with customized branding options for your invoices. Offers a free trial. Allows for tracking multiple projects, multiple clients, multiple contractors. http://www.freshbooks.com/

Basecamp Web-based project management and collaboration tool. Features include: To-dos, files, messages, schedules, and milestones. Offers a mobile version and a 30 day free trial. http://www.basecamphq.com/

Clientspot Online project management and time tracking tool developed with virtual assistants in mind. Features include: time and task tracking, file and calendar sharing, collaboration, conversation archives, client data tracking and more. Offers a 30 day free trial. http://www.myclientspot.com/

Paymo Online project management and invoicing software. Features include: free personal accounts, custom branded invoices, team tracking in professional accounts. http://www.paymo.biz/

Google Calendar Free online calendaring service. Features include email and pop-up event reminders, calendar sharing and syncing and more. https://accounts.google.com/calendar

OneNote Desktop planner and note taking software from Microsoft. Capture text, images, video and audio notes, and keep other important information readily available. http://www.office.microsoft.com/en-us/onenote/

Blogging Resources

WordPress.org WordPress is free, open source software you can use to create a full-featured website or blog. Blogs are hosted on your own domain. Complete documentation, tutorials, and a community support forum are provided to help users make the most of the WordPress software. http://wordpress.org/

WordPress.com Free blogs managed by the developers of the WordPress software. Includes custom design templates, integrated statistics, automatic spam protection and other features. Blogs are hosted at WordPress.com (not your own domain) http://wordpress.com/

<u>WordPress Widgets</u> A catalog of widgets created to expand and enhance WordPress.org blogs. Add everything from calendars to tag clouds, your IM status to stock quotes to your blog's sidebar. http://codex.wordpress.org/WordPress_Widgets

<u>Tumblr</u> Microblogging platform. Lets you easily share anything. Post text, photos, quotes, links, music, and videos, from your browser, phone, desktop, email, or wherever you happen to be. You can customize everything, from colors, to your theme's HTML. http://www.tumblr.com/

<u>Blog For Profit</u> Blog devoted to the topic of using a blog and social media to promote your business and create income. http://blogforprofit.com/

Email Resources

<u>Gmail</u> Free, full featured email accounts provided by Google. Features include message grouping by conversation, message un-send and more. http://www.gmail.com

<u>Mail2Web</u> Check and respond to your email from any computer, anywhere in the world, securely. http://www.mail2web.com/

<u>Jott</u> Voice-to-text service converts spoken messages to text and sends them to a specified destination via email, text message, or web update. http://www.jott.com

<u>Spam Arrest</u> Paid service, blocks spam from reaching your email inbox. http://www.spamarrest.com/

<u>Thunderbird</u> Free, full featured desktop email client. Features intelligent spam filter, built-in RSS readers and more. http://www.mozillamessaging.com/thunderbird

<u>Sanebox</u> Paid email filtering service designed to help save time by only putting important emails in your inbox (everything else goes to a folder you can access at any time.) http://www.sanebox.com/

File Sending, Conversion, Storage and Management

SendThisFile Easily send large and oversized files up to 2GB via this free online service. Recipient receives a download link via email. Also offers extended, paid features. http://www.sendthisfile.com/

Cute FTP Paid FTP (File Transfer Protocol) software that will allow you to access and update website files. Features include: multiple connections, drag and drop transfers and more. http://www.cuteftp.com/

Filezilla Free open source FTP software that will allow you to access and update website files. Features include support for large files, resume interrupted downloads, drag and drop, boomarks and more. http://filezilla-project.org/

Fetch For Mac users. Paid FTP software, offers multiple connections, drag and drop, resumption of interrupted downloads, file format conversion, and support for URLs. http://fetchsoftworks.com/

Dropbox Online backup, file sync, sharing, and storage service. 2GB online storage for free accounts. Sync files online and across your computers automatically. Share folders with multiple users, collaborate in real time. Mobile and web access. http://www.dropbox.com/

Zamzar Free online file conversion and sharing service. Convert documents, images, audio, video, eBooks and more. http://www.zamzar.com/

7zip Free, open-source file extractor and archiver. http://www.7-zip.org/

Universal Extractor Program designed to decompress and extract files from any type of archive or installer, such as ZIP or RAR files, self-extracting EXE files, application installers. Supports up to 50 different file formats. http://legroom.net/software/uniextract

Graphic and Website Design and Development

Logo Nerds Offers quality professional logos at incredibly inexpensive rates (as low as $27). A popular choice for logo design among startup virtual assistants. http://www.logonerds.com

WordPress.org WordPress is free, open source software you can use to create a full-featured website on your own domain. Complete documentation, tutorials, and a community support forum are provided to help users make the most of the WordPress software. http://wordpress.org/

ThemeForest Largest selection online of quality pre-designed themes and templates for use with WordPress websites and blogs. Prices range from $5 to $40. http://themeforest.net?ref=Codehead

GraphicRiver Buy and sell royalty-free, graphics, layered Photoshop files, vectors, icon packs, Adobe add-ons and design templates for just a few dollars. http://graphicriver.net?ref=Codehead

Zen Cart Free, user-friendly, open source shopping cart software. Features include newsletter manager, discount coupons, gift certificates, featured products, quantity discounts, multiple payment options, multiple shipping options, and more. http://www.zen-cart.com/

1ShoppingCart Full-featured shopping cart and ecommerce software. Features include: eCommerce websites, inventory management, order management, customer information, and marketing campaigns. http://www.1shoppingcart.com/

EJunkie Shopping cart software that allows you to sell downloads (and tangible goods) directly on your website. No setup fees and no transaction fees. http://www.e-junkie.com/

Google Webmaster Tools Provides detailed reports about your site's visibility on Google. See how Google crawls and indexes your site and learn about specific problems the SE has accessing it. View, classify, and download comprehensive data about internal and external links to your site. Find out which search queries drive traffic to your site, and more. http://www.google.com/webmasters/tools/

Bing Webmaster Tools Use the Bing Webmaster tools to improve your site's SEO, submit your sites and XML-based Sitemaps to Bing, get data on which pages of your site have been indexed, backlinks, inbound links and keyword performance. http://www.bing.com/toolbox/webmasters/

Google Analytics Lets you measure website traffic in detail – from keywords to exit pages, all the information you need to understand how users find, use and leave your site. Also can be used for tracking advertising ROI as well as track your Flash, video, and social networking sites and applications. http://www.google.com/analytics/

Komodo Edit Free open source editor. Supports multiple programming languages including HTML and PHP. http://www.activestate.com/komodo-edit

Newsletter Management Resources

<u>Mailchimp</u> Easy, affordable email marketing software. Features include: customizable templates, a selection of pre-made designer templates, integrates with social networks like Facebook, integrates with Google Analytics, RSS to email, autoresponders and more. http://www.mailchimp.com

<u>Constant Contact</u> Email marketing and survey marketing software. Free 60 day trial. Custom newsletter templates, drag and drop design, one-click editing, results tracking and more. http://www.constantcontact.com/

<u>Tribulant</u> WordPress Newsletter Plugin- collect emails, manage contacts, and send newsletters all with one feature-rich plugin. http://tribulant.com/plugins/view/1/wordpress-newsletter-plugin

<u>Aweber</u> Email marketing software. Features include: subscriber management, customized sign up forms, customized newsletter templates, autoresponder follow-up, blog-to-email, results tracking, and more. http://www.aweber.com

Phone, VOIP and Fax Resources

<u>Skype</u> VOIP (Voice Over Internet Protocol) software that you install on your computer and use to make and receive phone calls. Additional features include: voicemail, free Skype-to-Skype calls, video calls, conference calls, file sharing and more. http://www.skype.com

<u>FaxZero</u> Free online fax service. Send a document by fax up to three pages long anywhere in the US or Canada at no cost. http://faxzero.com/

<u>eFax</u> Paid online fax service with various levels of pricing. Send and receive faxes online. Choose your own fax number. http://www.efax.com/

<u>Google Voice</u> Enhances the existing capabilities of your phone, regardless of which phone or carrier you have - for free. Features include a central phone number, voice to text messaging, and free calls in the US and Canada. https://www.google.com/voice

<u>Oovoo</u> Video chat software allows for video conferencing with multiple callers. Additional features include the ability to record and send video messages, IM, embed a video chatroom in a website, share files up to 5MB, and more. http://www.oovoo.com/

Free Conference Calling Free conference call service can host up to 1,000 callers at a time and provides features such as recordable calls, line muting, call title and host announcement, guest speaker access and more. http://www.freeconferencecalling.com/

eVoice Feature-rich, paid virtual phone system. Features include auto attendant, call routing, voicemail-to-text, local and 1-800 numbers, and more. http://www.evoice.com/

Small Business Support

S.C.O.R.E. Small business mentoring and training. Provides free online and face-to-face business counseling, mentoring, training, and advice for small businesses just starting out. http://www.score.org/

IRS Small Business Center Get all the tax information and resources you need for your small business straight from the IRS. http://www.irs.gov/businesses/small/index.html

Small Business Administration Free support, information and resources to help you start, manage, and grow your small business. http://www.sba.gov/

Small Business Wiki Free wiki sourcebook of small business information and resources. http://smallbusiness.com/

National Association for the Self Employed Free online support system for self employed individuals. Also offers a paid membership with various benefits. Available free features include a Business Learning Center with videos and webinars, articles, podcasts and more. http://nase.org/

U.S. Chamber of Commerce Small Business Nation Online information resource includes a small business blog, business news and 'toolkits' for various industries. http://www.uschambersmallbusinessnation.com/

Small Business Dictionary Free, searchable online dictionary with definitions for more than 2,500 business terms. http://www.small-business-dictionary.org/

SBA Office of Entrepreneurial Development This Small Business Administration department helps small businesses start, grow and be competitive by providing training, counseling and other forms of management and technical assistance. http://www.sba.gov/about-offices-content/1/2463

Small Business Training Network The Small Business Training Network is a virtual campus provided by the Small Business Administration offering free training courses, workshops and informational resources designed to assist entrepreneurs and small business owners. http://www.sba.gov/category/navigation-structure/counseling-training

Social Networking Resources

Twitter Share status updates in 140 characters or less with your followers. Grow your following by following and interacting with fellow Tweeps with common interests, goals, or in your target market. Use Twitter as a marketing tool by tweeting useful resources and information. Considered one of the four core social networks a business must be active on. http://www.twitter.com

Facebook Create a Facebook page to help promote your business. Utilize Facebook's Q & A feature to help answer questions that showcase your skills and knowledge as a small business owner, virtual assistant, and within your niche. Grow your company's Facebook following and use the page to share exclusive information and interact with potential clients. Considered one of the four core social networks a business must be active on. http://www.facebook.com

LinkedIn Professional online network. Add your virtual assistant business to your LinkedIn profile. Use LinkedIn Groups to help grow your network, meet and interact with potential clients, and showcase your knowledge and skills. Considered one of the four core social networks a business must be active on. http://www.linkedin.com

Google+ Google calls it's business pages: *"A leap forward in building relationships between businesses and people."* Integrated with the Google +1 ranking system. Considered one of the four core social networks a business must be active on. http://www.google.com/+/business/

Pinterest An online social network built around virtual 'bulletin boards'. Allows users to collect, organize, and share things they find on the web. Foundationally visual – not a traditional social network – now with business pages! http://www.pinterest.com/

Biznik Online community of professionals and entrepreneurs. Create your profile, answer questions and network with other small business owners. Promote your own business, showcase your knowledge, and utilize the articles feature as part of your marketing plan. http://biznik.com/

Hootsuite Social media dashboard. Monitor keywords, manage multiple Twitter, Facebook, LinkedIn, Foursquare, Ping.fm and WordPress profiles, schedule messages, and more. http://hootsuite.com/

Tweetdeck Social media browser for staying in touch with what's happening on various social networks including Twitter and Facebook. http://www.tweetdeck.com/

More Small Business Resources

Echosign Online electronic signature service. Send contracts and agreements via email for quick, electronic signatures. Free and paid accounts. http://www.echosign.com/

e-SignLive Cloud-based electronic signature service. No software or hardware to purchase or install. Free and paid accounts. http://e-signlive.com/

Moodle Course Management System (CMS), also known as a Learning Management System (LMS) or a Virtual Learning Environment (VLE). Moodle is a free web application that educators can use to create effective online learning sites. http://moodle.org/

Screenhunter Free screen capture software. Grab full or partial screen shots from any screen or window on your computer. http://wisdom-soft.com/products/screenhunter_free.htm

LogMeIn Remote computer access service. Provide remote support, access and work on client files directly on their computer from the comfort of your own home office. https://secure.logmein.com/

PRWeb Paid press release distribution site. Features at different pricing levels include distribution to thousands of global media channels, SEO enhanced releases, live links, images, video and more. http://www.prweb.com/

PR Log Free press release distribution site. Features include live links in the body of the release, possibility of being picked up by Google News, video inclusion, and more. http://www.prlog.org/

OS Alt Find free open source alternatives to common, commercial software. Features software in multiple categories including: business, communications, databases, security, and web development. http://www.osalt.com/

The Entrepreneur's Handbook Compiled list of 101 online resources with links for first time entrepreneurs. Learn more about entrepreneurship, startups, small business, and much more. http://blog.kissmetrics.com/entrepreneurs-handbook/

Avast Free antivirus protection software – includes regular updates at no cost. Effectively blocks viruses and spyware, provides file reputation warnings. http://www.avast.com/free-antivirus-download

Eraser Free, advanced security tool for Windows which allows you to completely remove sensitive data from your computer's hard drive. http://www.heidi.ie/eraser/

Keepass Free, open source, light-weight, easy-to-use password manager. Save all of your passwords in one (locked and secure) Keepass database so you only have to remember one master password or select the key file to unlock and access your information. http://keepass.info/

Teamviewer Remote-access software allows you to remotely 'drive' any PC anywhere in the world (that you have permission to access). Useful for remote support services, team meetings, training sessions and more. http://www.teamviewer.com/

Anymeeting Free online audio and video conferencing service. Does not require registration or log in to join and participate in meetings. Host meetings, webinars, teleseminars, and more with up to 200 attendees for free (ad supported). Paid services also available. http://www.anymeeting.com

Documents

Worksheets

and

Sample Contracts

> On the following pages, you'll find these sample Worksheets,
> Business Documents and Sample Contracts / Agreements
> in the order shown in the list below.

Worksheets (6)

Success Plan Worksheet

Business Name Brainstorming Worksheet

Ideal Client Worksheet

Target Market Worksheet

Mission Statement Worksheet

Business Policies and Procedures
Worksheet

Business Documents (7)

Formal Business Plan Template

Invoice Template

UK Invoice Template (with VAT)

Web Design and Development Client
Questionnaire

Informal Late Payment Letter

Late Payment Collection Letter

Client Meeting Actionable Items Template

Sample Contracts and Agreements (22)

Virtual Assistant Services Agreement

Freelance Agreement (per hour)

Freelance Agreement (per project)

Canadian Services Contract (per hour)

Canadian Services Contract (per project)

UK Virtual Assistant Services Agreement

UK Services Contract (per hour)

UK Services Contract (per project)

Addendum to Contract

Mutual Release From Contract

Confidentiality Agreement

LLC Membership Agreement

Partnership Agreement

Partnership Dissolution Agreement

Website Design Contract

Project Management Contract

Ghostwriter Agreement

Consultant Services Agreement

UK Consultant Services Agreement

Cease and Desist Agreement

Agreement to Purchase Domain Name

Assignment of Copyright

Success Plan Worksheet
(Basic Informal Business Plan)

Section 1 – What are your goals?

_____

_____

_____

_____

_____

_____

_____

Section 2 - Why are you going into business?

_____

_____

_____

_____

_____

_____

_____

Section 3 – Who are your clients and where will you find them?

_____

_____

_____

_____

_____

_____

Section 4 – What services will you offer?

_____
_____
_____
_____
_____
_____
_____
_____
_____

Section 5 – Where will your business be located?

_____
_____
_____

Section 6 – When will you work?

_____
_____
_____

Section 7 – How much money will you make/spend?

_____
_____
_____
_____
_____

Section 8 – 5-year plan

_____
_____
_____
_____
_____
_____
_____
_____
_____

Section 9 – Exit strategy

_____
_____
_____
_____
_____
_____
_____
_____
_____

Section 10 – Additional Notes

_____
_____
_____
_____
_____

Business Name Brainstorming Worksheet

List *action words* related to the services you will provide. (For example, if you are offering transcription services you might choose: *type, transcribe, write, jot, etc.*)

_____   _____
_____   _____
_____   _____
_____   _____
_____   _____
_____   _____
_____   _____
_____   _____

List *descriptive words* that you feel apply to you as a service provider. (For example: *reliable, smart, savvy, virtual, etc.)*

_____   _____
_____   _____
_____   _____
_____   _____
_____   _____
_____   _____
_____   _____
_____   _____

List *generic business terms* that you might like to include.(For example: *classic, professional, solution(s), elite, personal(ized), etc.*)

_____   _____
_____   _____
_____   _____
_____   _____
_____   _____
_____   _____
_____   _____
_____   _____

List words that you simply *like the sound of.* (For example: *chic, viva, superb, opal, gauche, etc.*)

_____   _____
_____   _____
_____   _____
_____   _____
_____   _____
_____   _____
_____   _____

Don't forget to include the more obvious options in your list such as: your first and last name, your initials, the name of your city, town or state, the name of your street or neighborhood, and any other 'everyday' terms you think might work well as part of a business name.

_____   _____
_____   _____
_____   _____
_____   _____
_____   _____
_____   _____
_____   _____

Now that you've got your list, it's time to start playing around with the words to try to create a couple of business name options – remove or add words as you mix and match. Use a thesaurus, or visit Thesaurus.com, to discover additional related words (For example, *classic* might lead you to: *standard, superior, capital, champion, etc*). Keep putting the words together, brainstorming further, and mixing and matching until you come up with a business name you like!

_____
_____
_____
_____
_____
_____
_____
_____

Ideal Client Worksheet

Use your answers to the questions below to help you get clear on who your ideal client is. Remember, you can come back to the worksheet to update your answers and revise your definition at any time, and it's likely you'll do so at least once during your first year in business.

Don't add things that you *don't want* to the list - no sense putting your energy toward something negative. If you start to write "*My ideal client doesn't micromanage...*" focus on the positive aspect and write the opposite instead: "*My ideal client understands that I am a skilled professional, capable of managing the project from start to finish.*"

What type of industry would you enjoy being involved in?

_____

_____

_____

_____

_____

What size business do you want to work with?

_____

_____

_____

_____

_____

What stage of business development is your ideal client at?

_____

_____

_____

_____

What style of communication appeals to you?

_____

_____

_____

_____

What level of involvement in his/her own business does your ideal client have?

_____
_____
_____
_____
_____

What are your ideal client's demographics?

_____
_____
_____
_____
_____

Has your ideal client already had experience working with a virtual assistant?

_____
_____
_____
_____
_____

How does your ideal client view the role of a VA in his/her business?

_____
_____
_____
_____
_____

What kinds of services does your ideal client require?

_____
_____
_____
_____
_____

How many hours a week/month does your ideal client need from you?

_____

_____

_____

How savvy is your ideal client when it comes to the Internet, technology, etc.?

_____

_____

_____

_____

_____

_____

What else is important to you – what other attributes do you envision in an ideal client / an ideal working relationship?

_____

_____

_____

_____

_____

_____

_____

_____

_____

_____

_____

_____

_____

_____

_____

_____

Target Market Worksheet

Use the following questions to help you pinpoint your target markets

What specialized services are you offering?

_____

_____

_____

_____

_____

_____

_____

What problems do your services solve for potential clients?

_____

_____

_____

_____

_____

_____

_____

Which industries will best benefit from the use of your services? (and/or) Which industries are you interested in servicing?

_____

_____

_____

_____

_____

What is the average income for businesses operating in these industries?

(Use Google, The Small Business Administration website and other resources to locate some statistics – it's important to determine if the intended market can sustain your business. Only keep viable industries on your list.)

_____
_____
_____
_____
_____
_____
_____
_____
_____
_____
_____

Now, research and record possible advertising and networking opportunities for each viable industry.

Where do professionals in X industry spend time online?

(Include industry-specific forums, blogs, membership sites, social media sites, professional networks, and other types of online communities)

_____
_____
_____
_____
_____
_____
_____
_____
_____
_____

What newsletters, magazines and other feeds or publications are professionals in X industry reading and subscribing to?

_____

_____

_____

_____

_____

_____

Are there any offline events, conferences, conventions, retreats, etc. that professionals in X industry attend?

(Look for events you can either travel to locally, are worth considering long-distance travel to attend, or that you can participate in in some other way such as advertising, providing promotional items for 'goody bags', etc.)

_____

_____

_____

_____

_____

_____

How else can you share your message and business information with your target audience?

_____

_____

_____

_____

_____

If you've thoroughly answered all of the questions above, you've defined at least one target market and should have some good leads for where to begin implementing a marketing strategy for your virtual assistant business.

Mission Statement Worksheet

Answer the following questions and use your responses to craft your company mission statement.

What problem(s) does your company solve?

_____
_____
_____
_____
_____
_____
_____
_____

What pain point(s) do you address for your clients?

_____
_____
_____
_____
_____
_____
_____
_____

How is your VA business unique from all the other VA businesses?

_____
_____
_____
_____
_____
_____
_____
_____

Who is your target market?

_____

_____

_____

_____

_____

_____

What are your business goals?

_____

_____

_____

_____

_____

_____

What values does your company operate on?

_____

_____

_____

_____

_____

_____

What is your personal business philosophy?

_____

_____

_____

_____

_____

_____

Business Policies and Procedures Worksheet

Some points to consider when developing policies and procedures for your own virtual assistant business – jot down your notes and ideas as you work through these questions.

How will you handle the new client intake process?

_____
_____
_____
_____
_____
_____
_____
_____

How will you communicate with your clients?

_____
_____
_____
_____
_____
_____
_____
_____
_____

When will you be available to your clients?

_____
_____
_____
_____
_____
_____
_____
_____
_____

How will you manage your time?

_____

_____

_____

_____

_____

_____

How will you handle projects you are not qualified for?

_____

_____

_____

_____

_____

_____

How will you invoice your clients?

_____

_____

_____

_____

_____

_____

What types of payment will you accept?

_____

_____

_____

_____

_____

_____

How will you handle late payments and defaulted accounts?

_____
_____
_____
_____
_____
_____

How will you handle raising your rates?

_____
_____
_____
_____
_____
_____

How will you handle sensitive client information?

_____
_____
_____
_____
_____
_____

How will you ensure secure data storage?

_____
_____
_____
_____
_____
_____

What other issues can you imagine you'll need business policies and procedures in place to address?

_____

_____

_____

_____

_____

_____

_____

_____

_____

_____

_____

_____

_____

_____

_____

_____

_____

_____

_____

_____

_____

_____

_____

_____

_____

_____

_____

_____

Formal Business Plan Template

Using this outline and answering the following questions can help you draw up a professional business plan. Counseling centers can offer you guidance on your business plan. In addition, the business reference librarian at your local library can offer further assistance while you research information for your business plan.

<u>Cover Sheet</u>
Name of business, names of principals, address and phone number of business.

<u>Table of Contents</u>

E. For an Existing Business
   - Current Financial Statements Within Last 90 Days
   - Historical Financial Reports for Past Three Years
   - Balance Sheets for Past Three Years

IV. Supporting Documents
Personal resumes, job descriptions, personal financial statements, letters of reference, letters of intent, copies of leases, contracts, legal documents and anything else of relevance to the plan.

Questions

Description of Business

1. Business form: sole proprietorship, partnership, limited partnership, limited liability partnership, limited liability company, corporation ("S" corporation, "C" corporation, non-profit).

2. Merchandising, manufacturing, wholesale or service?

3. What is the product?

4. Is it a new business? A takeover? An expansion?

5. Why will your business be profitable?

6. When is your business open?

7. Is it a seasonal business?

8. What have you learned about your kind of business from outside sources (trade suppliers, banks, other business people, publications)?

The Market

9. Who exactly is your market? Define your market.

10. How are you going to satisfy your market wants?

11. How will you attract and hold your share of the market?

12. How are you going to price your product?

Competition

13. Who are your nearest competitors?

14. What is the financial condition of their business and the health of the industry in general?

15. What have you learned from their operations?

16. How do you plan to keep an eye on the competition?

Location of Business

17. What are your location needs?

18. What kind of building do you need?

19. Why is this a desirable area? A desirable building?

20. How do you plan to keep an eye on demographic shift in your area?

Management

21. How does your background/ business experience help you in this business? Also, for your benefit, what weaknesses do you have and how will you compensate for them (i.e., what related work experience have you had)?

22. Who is on the management team?

23. What are the duties of each individual on the management team?

24. Are these duties clearly defined? How?

25. What additional resources have you arranged to have available to help you and your business?

Personnel

26. What are your personnel needs now?

27. What will your needs be in five years?

28. What will be your wage scale: Salary or hourly? Overtime? Fringe benefits? Taxes?

29. How do you plan to train personnel for both operation and management?

Sources of Funding, Application and Expected Effect of Loan Investment

30. How will the loan (or other injection of new funds) make your business more profitable?

31. Should you buy or lease?

32. Do you need this new money? Establish a procedure for making borrowing decisions.

33. How is this loan to be used?

Your Company Name

Your Company Tagline or Service Guarantee

INVOICE

Street Address
City, ST ZIP Code
Phone 555.555.5555   Fax 555.555.5555

DATE: xx xx xxxx
INVOICE # 100
FOR: *Project or service description*

DUE DATE:

Bill To:
Name
Company Name
Street Address
City, State, ZIP Code
Phone

DESCRIPTION	AMOUNT
TOTAL	

Make all checks payable to **Your Company Name**
If you have any questions concerning this invoice, contact Name, Phone Number, E-mail

THANK YOU FOR YOUR BUSINESS!

INVOICE

Your company name/LOGO
Your address
Your contact details
Company #: {Company number}
VAT #: {VAT number}

Invoice Date:

Invoice No:

To:

Electronic Payment Details or Other Payment Processing Terms
(According to your own company policies and procedures)
XXXXXX Limited – A/C No. xxxxx– Sort Code: xx xx xx
Thank you for your business.

	SERVICES	**Amount £**
Date	Details	
	VAT @ 20%	
	Total	

	EXPENSES	**Amount £**
Date	Details	
	VAT @ 20%	
	Total	

INVOICE TOTAL

Contract work plus expenses detailed above.
Amount due: £XXXX

PAYMENT TERMS

Total due amount should be paid within _____ from the date of this invoice by bank transfer to account details above.

ENTER ANY ADDITIONAL PAYMENT TERMS AND POLICIES YOUR CONTRACTS INCLUDE HERE.

(Co name) registered in England No xxxxxxx
VAT Reg No xxxxxxx

Web Design & Development Client Questionnaire

Client Contact Information
Main Contact Name/Title:
Company Name:
Business Address:
Main Contact Email:
Main Contact Phone:
Fax:

General Company Information

How many decision makers at your company will be involved in / have input with the project?

Please tell us about your company. (Include information about your company services, products, location, target market, other demographics. If you have a current website and the 'About' page provides all of this information feel free to simply provide the URL.)

Do you have a current website? (Please provide URL and approximate date it was built.)

If this is a redesign project, please list what you DO like about your current website:

If this is a redesign project, please list what you DO NOT like about your current website:

Please describe your industry.

Who are your biggest competitors?

What do you like / dislike about their websites?

Design Preferences

Do you have any color preferences for your new site?

Do you have any imagery preferences for your new site?

Please list some websites you like, including URLs, and explain what you like about each.

Please list some websites you do NOT like and explain what you dislike about each.

Client Objective

What are your business objectives with the new / redesigned site? (For example: to promote the business, to sell products, to sell services, to provide a product catalog, to build membership, etc.)

Use a few adjectives to describe how the user should perceive the site. (For example: prestigious, friendly, fun, simple, innovative, experimental, cutting edge.)

Are there specific technologies (Flash, JavaScript, RSS, video, audio, etc.) that you would like to use in the site?

If so, in what ways do you feel these technologies will enhance user experience?

Additional Services Needed

Please refer to the list of services below and write 'yes' for services you believe or know you need. If you would like to provide additional information relative to services you believe or know you need, please include that here. Write 'no' for services you believe or know you do not need. If you have questions or would like to learn more about any of the services listed below, feel free to note this as well.

Tagline / slogan development –

Logo design / redesign –

Domain name registration –

Website hosting –

Traffic and visitor statistics reporting –

Search Engine Optimization (SEO) –

Online marketing –

Content creation / editing –

eCommerce (The ability to sell products online) –

Secure payment gateway (Process credit card payments) –

Website maintenance (Ongoing updates to the website) –

Update website content via the web (CMS – content management system) –

Blog, forum or other application –

Multimedia development (Video, audio, webinars, etc.) –

User management (User registration / log in / log out, etc.) –

Social media integration / marketing (Facebook, Twitter, Google+, LinkedIn, etc.) –

Other?

Marketing

Do you currently work with an advertising agency or public relations firm? –

Will they be involved in the development or redesign of your site? –

How do you intend to advertise or drive traffic to your site?

Describe your primary target audience (age, interests, income, education).

What are the key reasons why the target user chooses your products (cost, value, location, quality)?

Thank you for taking the time to answer these questions about your objectives for your website. We appreciate your interest in working with us and look forward to presenting our formal proposal on _____(Date). If you have questions, comments, or would like to add anything to the information you've provided here, don't hesitate to contact us.

YOUR COMPANY LOGO:

YOUR COMPANY NAME:_____

YOUR COMPANY CONTACT WEBSITE:_____

YOUR COMPANY CONTACT INFORMATION: _____

_____

YOUR BUSINESS NAME OR LOGO

Business Address
City, State and Zip Code
Business Phone Number
Business Email Address

Date
RE: Invoice #
Invoice Total:
Invoice Due Date:

Oops!

Salutation [Ex: To Whom It May Concern, Dear Client Name, Dear Company Name, etc.]

It appears you forgot to send us your payment in the amount of $[Insert amount due here] which was due on [Insert due date here].

We understand that as a busy [Enter friendly descriptive of client's position here - small business owner, entrepreneur, life coach, real estate agent, etc.] it can be all too easy to miss an invoice. Please take a moment to send us your payment today and, if it is already on its way to us, please accept our sincere thanks.

We appreciate your business!

Sincerely,

Your Name
Your Company Name
Your Contact Information

Attention: Accounts Payable
Re: Invoice#
Due Date:
Amount Due:
Interest or Late Payment Penalties Applied to Date:
TOTAL AMOUNT NOW DUE:

Salutation [Ex: To Whom It May Concern, Dear Client Name, Dear Company Name, etc.]

The above-mentioned invoice is currently past due. We need to reconcile this invoice and would appreciate your response at your earliest convenience.

If the payment in full has already been sent, please accept our sincere thanks and be sure to take a moment to let us know by which payment method you processed the invoice and on which date.

If the payment in full has not yet been sent, please take a moment to let us know when we can expect to receive payment and by which method. It's important to note that per the terms of our contract (noted below) your account is charged _____ [Insert your late payment penalty % or $ amount here] per _____ [Insert the terms by which late payment penalties are applied here – day/week/month, etc.] At this time you have incurred a late payment penalty of _____ [Insert current late payment penalty total here]

[Insert the late payment clause from your contract here.]

Attached, please find a copy of your updated invoice including the applicable late payment penalties.

Thank you in advance for your attention to this matter.

Sincerely,

Your Name
Your Company Name
Your Contact Information

Client Meeting Actionable Items Template

Subject	
Requested by	Date
	Time	Enter meeting time here
Location	Duration	
Attendees	
Follow up meeting?	

Key Points Discussed and Action Items

	Topic	Action Item(s)	Assigned to	Completion deadline
1				
2				
3				
4				
5				
6				
7				
8				
9				
10				

Virtual Assistant Services Agreement

This agreement is made effective as of XX CURRENT DATE XX by and between: CLIENT NAME, of CLIENT COMPANY NAME, CLIENT ADDRESS, CLIENT EMAIL and YOUR NAME, of YOUR COMPANY NAME, YOUR ADDRESS, YOUR EMAIL.

For the purpose of this agreement, the party who is contracting to receive services shall be referred to as "Client," and the party who will be providing the services shall be referred to as "Consultant." The Consultant has a substantial background in administrative assistance and is willing to provide services to the Client based on this background. The Client desires to have services provided by the Consultant. Therefore, the parties agree as follows:

Description of Services
Beginning on XX DATE XX, the Consultant will provide the following services (collectively, "Services") including but not limited to:

- Various Internet research tasks
  - Finding relevant links and articles for blog
  - Competitive industry research for client projects and for marketing
  - Stock photography/art research through various relevant websites
  - Compiling scheduling info for Seattle networking events
- Light Document Editing
  - Using Adobe and Office products as needed
- Project Management Assistance
- Various other services as agreed upon by both parties

The Consultant shall provide the Services in a timely manner as required by the client unless otherwise agreed upon by both parties.

Payment
The Consultant will provide Services to the Client at a rate of $XX.00 per working hour based on XX hours per month retainer rate. Payment will be made for the month in advance. The payment may be made monthly to the Consultant. The Consultant will provide the Client with a balance of hours on a time sheet on a weekly basis. Payment terms may change if agreed upon and signed by both the Client and the Consultant.

Outstanding Invoices-if applicable
In the event that the Client has an outstanding invoice, the charges shall accrue as follows (THIS IS A SAMPLE POLICY, EDIT THIS PORTION TO SUIT YOUR OWN COMPANY POLICIES):

30 days past due: 5 percent interest fee added to total amount owed

45 + days past due: The Consultant will cease all services and this agreement will be placed "on hold" until the Client has paid the total amount owed plus all applicable interest fees.

Reimbursement of Expenses

The Consultant shall be entitled to reimbursement for the following out-of-pocket expenses, if the Client expressly authorizes the expenses ahead of time. (Copies of all receipts will be provided to the Client to substantiate reimbursement of expenses.)

- Postage
- Delivery/Shipping Fees
- Copying
- Printing and artwork
- Project-related long-distance telephone calls
- Other authorized expenses purchased solely for the Client

Support Services

At this time, no support staff is needed for the Client's projects. Should the need arise, the Client will be informed ahead of time that outsourcing or sub-contracting may be required. The Client and the Consultant will discuss options as the need arises.

Term/Termination

This agreement shall be effective until either party terminates the agreement by providing thirty (30) days written notice to the other party.

Relationship of Parties

It is understood by both parties that the Consultant is an Independent Contractor and is not an Employee of the Client. The Client will not provide tax payments or benefits, including health insurance, paid vacation or any other Employee benefit for the Consultant.

Confidentiality

The Client recognizes that the Consultant has and will have the following proprietary information:

- Products
- Prices
- Costs
- Discounts
- Future plans
- Contacts database
- Business affairs, policies, procedures
- Personal and/or financial information
- Other information (collectively "Information") which are valuable, special and unique assets of the Client.

The Consultant agrees not to, at any time or in any manner, either directly or indirectly, use any Information for Consultant's own benefit, or divulge, disclose, or communicate in any manner any Information to any third party without the prior written consent of the Client. The Consultant will protect the Information and treat it as strictly confidential. A violation of this article shall be a material violation of this Agreement.

Confidentiality After Termination

The confidentiality provisions of this Agreement shall remain in full force and effect after the termination of this Agreement.

Return of Records

Upon termination of this Agreement, the Consultant shall deliver all records, notes, data, memoranda, models and equipment of any nature that are in the Consultant's possession or under the Consultant's control and that are the Client's property or relate to the Client's business.

Entire Agreement

This Agreement contains the entire agreement of the parties and there are no other promises or conditions in any other agreement, whether oral or written. This Agreement supersedes any prior written or oral agreement between the parties.

Amendment

This Agreement may be modified or amended if the amendment is made in writing and is signed by both parties.

Notices

All notices required or permitted under the Agreement shall be in writing and shall be deemed delivered when delivered by facsimile, in person, or deposited in the United States mail, postage prepaid, to the intended party's current mailing address.

Both parties will alert the other of a change in contact information.

Severability

If any provision of this Agreement shall be held to be invalid or unenforceable for any reason, the remaining provisions shall continue to be valid and enforceable. If a court finds that any provision of the Agreement is invalid or unenforceable, but that by limiting such provisions, it would become valid and enforceable, then such provision shall be deemed to be written, construed and enforced as so limited.

Waiver of Contractual Right

The failure of either party to enforce any provision of this Agreement shall not be construed as a waiver or limitation of that party's right to subsequently enforce and compel strict compliance with every provision of this Agreement.

Applicable Law

This Agreement shall be governed by the laws of the State of YOUR STATE, the Consultant's state of business registration.

Client Signature_____   Date_____

Consultant Signature_____   Date_____

Freelance Agreement – per hour

This Agreement is made this ___ day of ____ 20__, between <u>YOUR COMPANY</u>, having it's principal place of business at _____, and <u>THEIR COMPANY</u> having their principal place of business at <u>Company's address including country</u>. In consideration of <u>Company Name</u> retaining YOUR COMPANY to conduct an independent service for <u>Company Name</u> it is agreed as follows:

1. Compensation and Terms

<u>Company Name</u> hereby retains YOUR COMPANY and YOUR COMPANY hereby agrees to perform the following services:

- YOUR COMPANY will perform the following jobs:
  - X SERVICES as specified by <u>Company Name</u>.
    - This will include the following actions:
      1.
      2.
      3.
      4.

  - <u>Company Name</u> will provide the following deliverables:
      1.
      2.
      3.
      4.

  - Time Detail:
      1. YOUR COMPANY will begin the <u>Company PROJECT</u> upon the completion of this contract, and having received a deposit of $X00.00, as well as the necessary client deliverables as described above.

      2. *Further info on expected process of project if needed – enter your own text here.*

      3. YOUR COMPANY will not be held responsible for delays in project completion resulting from client or third party delays.

- The following fees shall apply:
    1. $X00.00 deposit to begin project
    2. $X.00 per hour until completion of COMPANY PROJECT. Any additional projects will require an additional contract.

- Invoicing and payment:
    1. Invoices shall be sent to THEIR COMPANY NAME every ___ days via _____ and are due and payable on Net 14 terms.
    2. Invoices not reconciled within 14 days incur a $____ late payment penalty.
    3. Invoices not reconciled within 30 days incur a $____ late payment penalty.
    4. Invoices not reconciled more than 30 days *(YOU MUST CREATE your own policy here – determine how you will handle these situations. This is why a deposit is important!)*
    5. Invoices are payable via the following methods: (list your accepted payment methods.)

2. Confidentiality

This Agreement creates a confidential relationship between YOUR COMPANY and Company Name. Information concerning YOUR COMPANY and/or Company Name business affairs, vendors, finances, properties, methods of operation, computer programs, employees, documentation, and other such information whether written, oral, or otherwise, is confidential in nature. YOUR COMPANY, Company Name and employees of both will adhere fully to this confidentiality agreement for the duration of this contract and beyond.

3. Governing law

This agreement shall be binding upon the heirs and assigns of the parties and shall be governed by and interpreted according to the laws of the State of _____.

4. Entire agreement

This agreement represents the full understanding between the parties and there is no other agreement, oral or written, between them, and that this agreement may not be modified without an agreement in writing signed by the party to be charged. This contract is in effect until written notification of termination from either party.

5. Notices

All notices or other documents under this agreement shall be in writing and delivered personally or fax received, or mailed by certified mail, postage prepaid, addressed to YOUR COMPANY and Company Name at their last known addresses.

6. Single Points of Contact *(if necessary...this is useful when contracting large corporations with multiple departments and levels of executives and their assistants)*

YOUR COMPANY's single point of contact will be YOUR NAME (email@yourdomain.com). Company Name's single point of contact will be Contact Name (email@website.com). All correspondence concerning the project will be handled between YOUR NAME and Contact Name. All correspondence sent from other employee's of the company will be ignored and forwarded to the respective single point of contact.

In the event that either YOUR NAME or Contact Name are no longer with their respective companies a new single point of contact will be assigned in writing immediately.

7. Non-Competition

Both YOUR COMPANY and Company Name agree to non-competition regarding their respective customers. Neither company will attempt to take any customers from the other company for any reason whatsoever. Any client information will be kept confidential between the companies and will be used for the sole purpose of performing the contractual services as herein defined in this document.

8. Source Files and Copyrights

Company Name will retain all source files for all projects completed by YOUR COMPANY including their copyrights.

9. Agreement Timeout

Company Name is responsible for supplying all needed content to YOUR COMPANY by Mutually Agreed Upon Date. If Company Name does not provide the full content by Mutually Agreed Upon Date, Company Name will incur a late fee of _____ and will be given a month to supply the rest of the content. If Company Name does not supply the content, then the contract agreement between Company Name and YOUR COMPANY will become void.

ACCEPTED AND AGREED:

YOUR COMPANY   Company Name

BY: BY:

_____   _____
(signature)   (signature)

_____   _____
(Print Name)   (Print Name)

Date:_____   Date: _____

Freelance Agreement – per project

This Agreement is made this ___ day of ____ 20__, between <u>YOUR COMPANY</u>, having it's principal place of business at _____, and <u>THEIR COMPANY</u> having their principal place of business at <u>Company's address including country</u>. In consideration of <u>Company Name</u> retaining YOUR COMPANY to conduct an independent service for <u>Company Name</u> it is agreed as follows:

1. **Compensation and Terms**
   <u>Company Name</u> hereby retains YOUR COMPANY and YOUR COMPANY hereby agrees to perform the following services:

   - YOUR COMPANY will perform the following jobs:

     - X SERVICES as specified by <u>Company Name</u>.

       - This will include the following actions:

         1.
         2.
         3.
         4.

   - <u>Company Name</u> will provide the following deliverables:

         1.
         2.
         3.
         4.

   - Time Detail:

       1. YOUR COMPANY will begin the <u>Company PROJECT</u> upon the completion of this contract, and having received a deposit of $X00.00, as well as the necessary client deliverables as described above.

       2. [--Further info on expected process of project if needed – enter your own text here.--]

       3. YOUR COMPANY will not be held responsible for delays in project completion resulting from client or third party delays.

- The following fees shall apply:
    1. $X00.00 deposit to begin project
    2. $X00.00 payment upon approval of completed project by Company Name.
    3. $X.00 per hour for future work related to COMPANY PROJECT. Any additional projects will require an additional contract.

2. Confidentiality
This Agreement creates a confidential relationship between YOUR COMPANY and Company Name. Information concerning YOUR COMPANY and/or Company Name business affairs, vendors, finances, properties, methods of operation, computer programs, employees, documentation, and other such information whether written, oral, or otherwise, is confidential in nature. YOUR COMPANY, Company Name and employees of both will adhere fully to this confidentiality agreement for the duration of this contract and beyond.

3. Governing law
This agreement shall be binding upon the heirs and assigns of the parties and shall be governed by and interpreted according to the laws of the State of _____.

4. Entire agreement
This agreement represents the full understanding between the parties and there is no other agreement, oral or written, between them, and that this agreement may not be modified without an agreement in writing signed by the party to be charged. This contract is in effect until written notification of termination from either party.

5. Notices
All notices or other documents under this agreement shall be in writing and delivered personally or fax received, or mailed by certified mail, postage prepaid, addressed to YOUR COMPANY and Company Name at their last known addresses.

6. Single Points of Contact *(if necessary…this is useful when contracting large corporations with multiple departments and levels of executives and their assistants)*
YOUR COMPANY's single point of contact will be YOUR NAME (email@yourdomain.com). Company Name's single point of contact will be Contact Name (email@website.com). All correspondence concerning the project will be handled between YOUR NAME and Contact Name. All correspondence sent from other employee's of the company will be ignored and forwarded to the respective single point of contact.

In the event that either YOUR NAME or Contact Name are no longer with their respective companies a new single point of contact will be assigned in writing immediately.

7. Non-Competition
Both YOUR COMPANY and Company Name agree to non-competition regarding their respective customers. Neither company will attempt to take any customers from the other company for any reason whatsoever. Any client information will be kept confidential between the companies and will be used for the sole purpose of performing the contractual services as herein defined in this document.

8. Source Files and Copyrights
Company Name will retain all project source files including their copyrights.

9. Agreement Timeout

Company Name is responsible for supplying all needed content to YOUR COMPANY by Mutually Agreed Upon Date. If Company Name does not provided the full content by Mutually Agreed Upon Date, Company Name will incur a late fee of _____ and will be given a month to supply the rest of the content. If Company Name does not supply the content, then the contract agreement between Company Name and YOUR COMPANY will become void.

ACCEPTED AND AGREED:

YOUR COMPANY   Company Name

BY: BY:

_____   _____
(signature)   (signature)

_____   _____
(Print Name)   (Print Name)

Date:_____   Date: _____

CANADIAN SERVICES CONTRACT
(per hour)

This agreement is made effective as of **[___ DATE ___]**

By and between: **[___ Client Name ___]**

CLIENT NAME / COMPANY NAME
CLIENT ADDRESS
CLIENT PHONE

and **[___ Your Name / Your Company Name ___]**
YOUR NAME / COMPANY NAME
YOUR BUSINESS ADDRESS
YOUR BUSINESS PHONE

In this agreement, the party who is contracting to receive services shall be referred to as "Client," and the party who will be providing the services shall be referred to as "Contractor."

1. The purpose of this contract is to outline the conditions of provision of services by the Contractor to the Client. The Contractor (its associates and sub-contractors, collectively the "Contractor") will provide the following services to the Client:

    See Schedule "A" attached.

2. The Contractor agrees that all products or results arising out of the performance of the services, including but not limited to data, information and intellectual property including copyrightable materials and inventions, shall be the exclusive property of the Client and shall be provided promptly to the Client. The Contractor shall retain no rights in or to such products or results.

3. The parties agree that this contract is on a fee-for-service basis and in no way whatsoever constitutes an employment relationship. At no time will the Contractor be considered an employee of the Client. In particular, but without limiting the generality of the foregoing,

    (a) The parties agree that the Contractor will not be entitled to any employee benefits from the Client, including but not limited to pension or health benefits or insurance coverage.

(b) The parties agree that the Client has no liabilities whatsoever arising from this contract under provincial employment legislation, including but not restricted to employment standards legislation, workplace safety legislation, worker's compensation legislation, labour relations legislation, or human rights legislation. The Contractor specifically acknowledges that it has no right to make a claim through the Client to a worker's safety/insurance board for injuries arising out of performance of services under this Agreement.

(d) The parties agree that the Client has no liabilities whatsoever arising from this contract under federal legislation including but not restricted to the *Income Tax Act, Canada Pension Plan,* or the *Employment Insurance Act.* The Contractor specifically acknowledges that it is solely responsible for payment of all applicable income taxes or contributions on fees paid for the services.

4. The Client agrees to pay the Contractor a fixed fee basis of $XXX [in Canadian currency per hour plus] GST if applicable, upon receipt of an invoice from the Contractor. The Client has chosen to retain the Contractor's services on an hourly rather than a retainer basis and acknowledges that retainer clients' requirements take priority over hourly contracts. The Client may move from an hourly basis to a retainer basis at any time he or she desires. The Contractor will provide the Client with a GST number if he/she is charging GST on fees. The Contractor will invoice the Client on a [*weekly/monthly/quarterly* basis].

5. The parties agree that all incidental expenses incurred by the Contractor on behalf of the client will be invoiced to the Client.

6. The Contractor acknowledges that it, in the course of carrying out the services, may be in receipt of confidential information including but not limited to Client materials, records, memoranda and other documents, and personal information about individuals. The Contractor agrees that it shall not at any time during or after the term of this Agreement:

    (a) use the confidential information for any purpose other than the provision of the services specified in this Agreement; or

    (b) deliberately or negligently disclose such confidential information to anyone other than Contractor's employees and agents with a need to know such confidential information, who have agreed in writing to keep confidential the information in accordance with the terms of this Agreement. Contractor may also disclose confidential information with the written permission of the Client, or as required by law. On the request of the Client, when invoices to date have been paid in full, the Contractor will promptly return all materials and documents that the Client has provided.

7. Neither party shall use, or authorize others to use, the name, symbols, or marks of the other party or that party's employees or agents in any advertising or publicity material or make any form of representation or statement that would constitute an express or implied endorsement by the other party of any commercial product or service, without prior written approval from that other party whose name, symbol or marks is to be used.

8. This Agreement may be terminated by either party giving thirty (30) days written notice to the other.

9. The parties to this Agreement are independent contractors. Nothing contained herein shall be deemed or construed to create between the parties hereto a partnership or joint venture or employment or principal-agent relationship. No party shall have the authority to act on behalf of any other party or to bind another party in any manner.

10. This Agreement contains the entire understanding between the parties and supersedes any previous understandings or agreements, written or otherwise, concerning this matter. It may be modified only by the written agreement of the parties.

IN WITNESS WHEREOF the parties have executed this Agreement. Each individual signing for a corporation hereby personally warrants his or her legal authority to bind that corporation.

Client: **Contractor:**

Name: _____   Name: _____

Title: _____   Title _____

SCHEDULE "A"
<u>SCOPE OF SERVICES</u>

List the services you are being contracted to provide to the client here in Schedule "A"

CANADIAN SERVICES CONTRACT
(per project)

This agreement is made effective as of **[___ DATE ___]**

By and between: **[___ Client Name ___]**
CLIENT NAME / COMPANY NAME
CLIENT ADDRESS
CLIENT PHONE

and **[___ Your Name / Your Company Name ___]**
YOUR NAME / COMPANY NAME
YOUR BUSINESS ADDRESS
YOUR BUSINESS PHONE

In this agreement, the party who is contracting to receive services shall be referred to as "Client," and the party who will be providing the services shall be referred to as "Contractor."

1. The purpose of this contract is to outline the conditions of provision of services by the Contractor to the Client. The Contractor (its associates and sub-contractors, collectively the "Contractor") will provide the following services to the Client:

    See Schedule "A" attached.

2. The Contractor agrees that all products or results arising out of the performance of the services, including but not limited to data, information and intellectual property including copyrightable materials and inventions, shall be the exclusive property of the Client and shall be provided promptly to the Client. The Contractor shall retain no rights in or to such products or results.

3. The parties agree that this contract is on a fee-for-service basis and in no way whatsoever constitutes an employment relationship. At no time will the Contractor be considered an employee of the Client. In particular, but without limiting the generality of the foregoing,

    (a) The parties agree that the Contractor will not be entitled to any employee benefits from the Client, including but not limited to pension or health benefits or insurance coverage.

(b) The parties agree that the Client has no liabilities whatsoever arising from this contract under provincial employment legislation, including but not restricted to employment standards legislation, workplace safety legislation, worker's compensation legislation, labour relations legislation, or human rights legislation. The Contractor specifically acknowledges that it has no right to make a claim through the Client to a worker's safety/insurance board for injuries arising out of performance of services under this Agreement.

(d) The parties agree that the Client has no liabilities whatsoever arising from this contract under federal legislation including but not restricted to the *Income Tax Act, Canada Pension Plan,* or the *Employment Insurance Act.* The Contractor specifically acknowledges that it is solely responsible for payment of all applicable income taxes or contributions on fees paid for the services.

4. The Client agrees to pay the Contractor a fixed fee basis of $____ in ____ currency per hour plus applicable taxes, upon receipt of an invoice from the Contractor. [The Contractor will provide the Client with a GST number if he/she is charging GST on fees. ***Amend depending on jurisdiction***] Upon the signing of this contract the Client will provide the Contractor with a deposit in the amount of 50% of the total estimated project fees. Thereafter, the Contractor will provide an invoice and statement to the Client on a [weekly] basis.

5. The parties agree that all incidental expenses incurred by the Contractor on behalf of the client will be invoiced to the Client.

6. The Contractor acknowledges that it, in the course of carrying out the services, may be in receipt of confidential information including but not limited to Client materials, records, memoranda and other documents, and personal information about individuals. The Contractor agrees that it shall not at any time during or after the term of this Agreement:

(a) use the confidential information for any purpose other than the provision of the services specified in this Agreement; or

(b) deliberately or negligently disclose such confidential information to anyone other than Contractor's employees and agents with a need to know such confidential information, who have agreed in writing to keep confidential the information in accordance with the terms of this Agreement. Contractor may also disclose confidential information with the written permission of the Client, or as required by law. On the request of the Client and when invoices have been paid in full to date, the Contractor will promptly return all materials and documents that the Client has provided.

7. Neither party shall use, or authorize others to use, the name, symbols, or marks of the other party or that party's employees or agents in any advertising or publicity material or make any form of representation or statement that would constitute an express or implied endorsement by the other party of any commercial product or service, without prior written approval from that other party whose name, symbol or marks is to be used.

8. This Agreement may be terminated by either party giving thirty (30) days written notice to the other.

9. The parties to this Agreement are independent contractors. Nothing contained herein shall be deemed or construed to create between the parties hereto a partnership or joint venture or employment or principal-agent relationship. No party shall have the authority to act on behalf of any other party or to bind another party in any manner.

10. This Agreement contains the entire understanding between the parties and supersedes any previous understandings or agreements, written or otherwise, concerning this matter. It may be modified only by the written agreement of the parties.

IN WITNESS WHEREOF the parties have executed this Agreement. Each individual signing for a corporation hereby personally warrants his or her legal authority to bind that corporation.

Client: **Contractor:**

Name: _____   Name: _____

Title: _____   Title _____

SCHEDULE "A"
SCOPE OF SERVICES

Fully detail the specifications of the project you are being contracted to complete here.

YOUR BUSINESS NAME OR LOGO
Business Address
Business Phone Number
Business Email Address
Company #: {Company number}; VAT #: {VAT number}

UK Virtual Assistant Services Agreement

THIS AGREEMENT is made this [ENTER DATE] day of [ENTER YEAR]

BETWEEN:

Client Name
Client Address
(registered address if a registered company)
Company No.

hereinafter called "the Client"

and

Your Name / Your Company Name
whose registered office is (if applicable)
Your Company Address
Company No.

hereinafter called "the Contractor".

The Consultant has a substantial background in administrative assistance and is willing to provide services to the Client based on this background. The Client desires to have services provided by the Consultant. Therefore, the parties agree as follows:

Description of Services
Beginning on XX DATE XX the Consultant will provide the following services (collectively, "Services") including but not limited to:

- Various Internet research tasks
  - Finding relevant links and articles for blog
  - Competitive industry research for client projects and for marketing
  - Stock photography/art research through various relevant websites
  - Compiling scheduling info for XXX networking events
- Light Document Editing
  - Using Adobe and Office products as needed
- Project Management Assistance
- Various other services as agreed upon by both parties
- ENTER YOUR OWN SERVICES IN THIS SPACE!

The Consultant shall provide the Services in a timely manner as required by the client unless otherwise agreed upon by both parties.

Payment

The Consultant will provide Services to the Client at a rate of £XX.00 per working hour plus VAT if applicable based on XX hours per month retainer rate. Payment will be made for the month in advance. The payment may be made monthly to the Consultant. The Consultant will provide the Client with a balance of hours on a time sheet on a weekly basis. Payment terms may change if agreed upon and signed by both the Client and the Consultant.

Outstanding Invoices-if applicable

In the event that the Client has an outstanding invoice, the charges shall accrue as follows (THIS IS A SAMPLE POLICY, EDIT THIS PORTION TO SUIT YOUR OWN COMPANY POLICIES):

30 days past due: 5 percent interest fee added to total amount owed

45 + days past due: The Consultant will cease all services and this agreement will be placed "on hold" until the Client has paid the total amount owed plus all applicable interest fees.

Reimbursement of Expenses

The Consultant shall be entitled to reimbursement for the following out-of-pocket expenses, if the Client expressly authorises the expenses ahead of time. (Copies of all receipts will be provided to the Client to substantiate reimbursement of expenses.)

- Postage
- Delivery/Postage Fees
- Copying
- Printing and artwork
- Project-related long-distance telephone calls
- Other authorised expenses purchased solely for the Client

Support Services

At this time, no support staff is needed for the Client's projects. Should the need arise, the Client will be informed ahead of time that outsourcing or sub-contracting may be required. The Client and the Consultant will discuss options as the need arises.

Term/Termination

This agreement shall be effective until either party terminates the agreement by providing thirty (30) days written notice to the other party.

Relationship of Parties

It is understood by both parties that the Consultant is an Independent Contractor and is not an Employee of the Client. The Client will not provide tax payments or benefits, including health insurance paid holiday or any other Employee benefit for the Consultant.

Confidentiality

The Client recognises that the Consultant has and will have the following proprietary information:

- Products
- Prices
- Costs
- Discounts
- Future plans
- Contacts database
- Business affairs, policies, procedures
- Personal and/or financial information
- Other information (collectively "Information") which are valuable special and unique assets of the Client.

The Consultant agrees not to at any time or in any manner either directly or indirectly use any Information for the Consultant's own benefit, or divulge disclose or communicate in any manner any Information to any third party without the prior written consent of the Client. The Consultant will protect the Information and treat it as strictly confidential. A violation of this article shall be a material violation of this Agreement.

Confidentiality After Termination

The confidentiality provisions of this Agreement shall remain in full force and effect after the termination of this Agreement.

Return of Records

Upon termination of this Agreement the Consultant shall deliver all records, notes, data, memoranda, models and equipment of any nature that are in the Consultant's possession or under the Consultant's control and that are the Client's property or relate to the Client's business.

Entire Agreement

This Agreement contains the entire agreement of the parties and there are no other promises or conditions in any other agreement, whether oral or written. This Agreement supersedes any prior written or oral agreement between the parties.

Amendment

This Agreement may be modified or amended if the amendment is made in writing and is signed by both parties.

Notices

All notices required or permitted under the Agreement shall be in writing and shall be deemed delivered when delivered by facsimile in person or deposited in the United Kingdom mail service postage prepaid to the intended party's current mailing address.

Both parties will alert the other of a change in contact information.

Severability

If any provision of this Agreement shall be held to be invalid or unenforceable for any reason, the remaining provisions shall continue to be valid and enforceable. If a court finds that any provision of the Agreement is invalid or unenforceable but that by limiting such provisions it would become valid and enforceable, then such provision shall be deemed to be written construed and enforced as so limited.

Waiver of Contractual Right

The failure of either party to enforce any provision of this Agreement shall not be construed as a waiver or limitation of that party's right to subsequently enforce and compel strict compliance with every provision of this Agreement.

Applicable Law

This Agreement shall be governed by the laws of the United Kingdom

Client Signature_____

Date_____

Consultant Signature_____

Date_____

UK Services Contract (per hour)

THIS AGREEMENT is made this [ENTER DATE] day of [ENTER YEAR]

BETWEEN:

Client Name
Client Address
(registered address if a registered company)
Company No.

hereinafter called "the Client"

and

Your Name / Your Company Name
whose registered office is (if applicable)
Your Company Address
Company No.

hereinafter called "the Contractor".

1. The purpose of this contract is to outline the conditions of provision of services by the Contractor to the Client. The Contractor (its associates and sub-contractors collectively "the Contractor") will provide the following services to the Client:

   See Schedule "A" attached.

2. The Contractor agrees that all products or results arising out of the performance of the services including but not limited to data information and intellectual property including copyrightable materials and inventions shall be the exclusive property of the Client and shall be provided promptly to the Client. The Contractor shall retain no rights in or to such products or results.

3. The parties agree that this contract is on a fee-for-service basis and in no way whatsoever constitutes an employment relationship. At no time will the Contractor be considered an employee of the Client. In particular but without limiting the generality of the foregoing:

(a) The parties agree that the Contractor will not be entitled to any employee benefits from the Client, including but not limited to pension or health benefits or insurance coverage.

(b) The parties agree that the Client has no liabilities whatsoever arising from this contract under provincial employment legislation, including but not restricted to employment standards legislation, workplace safety legislation worker's compensation legislation, labour relations legislation or human rights legislation. The Contractor specifically acknowledges that it has no right to make a claim through the Client to a worker's safety/insurance board for injuries arising out of performance of services under this Agreement.

(c) The parties agree that the Client has no liabilities whatsoever arising from this contract under United Kingdom legislation. The Contractor specifically acknowledges that it is solely responsible for payment of all applicable income taxes or contributions on fees paid for the services.

4. The Client agrees to pay the Contractor a fixed fee basis of £XXX per hour plus VAT if applicable upon receipt of an invoice from the Contractor. The Client has chosen to retain the Contractor's services on an hourly rather than a retainer basis and acknowledges that retainer clients' requirements take priority over hourly contracts. The Client may move from an hourly basis to a retainer basis at any time he or she desires. The Contractor will invoice the Client on a [weekly / monthly / quarterly] basis.

5. The parties agree that all incidental expenses incurred by the Contractor on behalf of the client will be invoiced to the Client.

6. The Contractor acknowledges that it, in the course of carrying out the services, may be in receipt of confidential information including but not limited to Client materials records memoranda and other documents and personal information about individuals. The Contractor agrees that it shall not at any time during or after the term of this Agreement:

(a) use the confidential information for any purpose other than the provision of the services specified in this Agreement; or

(b) deliberately or negligently disclose such confidential information to anyone other than Contractor's employees and agents with a need to know such confidential information who have agreed in writing to keep confidential the information in accordance with the terms of this Agreement. Contractor may also disclose confidential information with the written permission of the Client or as required by law. On the request of the Client, when invoices to date have been paid in full the Contractor will promptly return all materials and documents that the Client has provided.

7. Neither party shall use or authorize others to use the name symbols or marks of the other party or that party's employees or agents in any advertising or publicity material or make any form of representation or statement that would constitute an express or implied endorsement by the other party of any commercial product or service without prior written approval from that other party whose name symbol or marks is to be used.

8. This Agreement may be terminated by either party giving thirty (30) days written notice to the other.

9. The parties to this Agreement are independent contractors. Nothing contained herein shall be deemed or construed to create between the parties hereto a partnership or joint venture or employment or principal-agent relationship. No party shall have the authority to act on behalf of any other party or to bind another party in any manner.

10. This Agreement contains the entire understanding between the parties and supersedes any previous understandings or agreements written or otherwise concerning this matter. It may be modified only by the written agreement of the parties.

IN WITNESS WHEREOF the parties hereto have hereunto executed this Agreement the day and year first before written. Each individual signing for a corporation hereby personally warrants his or her legal authority to bind that corporation.

Client: **Contractor:**

Name: _____   **Name:** _____

Title: _____   **Title:** _____

SCHEDULE "A"
SCOPE OF SERVICES

List the services you are being contracted to provide to the client here in Schedule "A"

UK Services Contract (per project)

THIS AGREEMENT is made this [ENTER DATE] day of [ENTER YEAR]

BETWEEN:

Client Name
Client Address
(registered address if a registered company)
Company No.

hereinafter called "the Client"

and

Your Name / Your Company Name
whose registered office is (if applicable)
Your Company Address
Company No.

hereinafter called "the Contractor".

1. The purpose of this contract is to outline the conditions of provision of services by the Contractor to the Client. The Contractor (its associates and sub-contractors, collectively "the Contractor") will provide the following services to the Client:

   See Schedule "A" attached.

2. The Contractor agrees that all products or results arising out of the performance of the services including but not limited to data information and intellectual property including copyrightable materials and inventions shall be the exclusive property of the Client and shall be provided promptly to the Client. The Contractor shall retain no rights in or to such products or results.

3. The parties agree that this contract is on a fee-for-service basis and in no way whatsoever constitutes an employment relationship. At no time will the Contractor be considered an employee of the Client. In particular but without limiting the generality of the foregoing:

(a) The parties agree that the Contractor will not be entitled to any employee benefits from the Client including but not limited to pension or health benefits or insurance coverage.

(b) The parties agree that the Client has no liabilities whatsoever arising from this contract under provincial employment legislation including but not restricted to employment standards legislation workplace safety legislation worker's compensation legislation labour relations legislation or human rights legislation. The Contractor specifically acknowledges that it has no right to make a claim through the Client to a worker's safety/insurance board for injuries arising out of performance of services under this Agreement.

(c) The parties agree that the Client has no liabilities whatsoever arising from this contract under United Kingdom legislation. The Contractor specifically acknowledges that it is solely responsible for payment of all applicable income taxes or contributions on fees paid for the services.

4. The Client agrees to pay the Contractor a fixed fee basis of £XXX per hour plus VAT if applicable upon receipt of an invoice from the Contractor. [The Contractor will provide the Client with a VAT number if he/she is charging VAT on fees. *Amend depending on jurisdiction*] Upon the signing of this contract the Client will provide the Contractor with a deposit in the amount of 50% of the total estimated project fees. Thereafter the Contractor will provide an invoice and statement to the Client on a [weekly] basis.

5. The parties agree that all incidental expenses incurred by the Contractor on behalf of the client will be invoiced to the Client.

6. The Contractor acknowledges that in the course of carrying out the services it may be in receipt of confidential information including but not limited to Client materials records memoranda and other documents and personal information about individuals. The Contractor agrees that it shall not at any time during or after the term of this Agreement:

(a) use the confidential information for any purpose other than the provision of the services specified in this Agreement; or

(b) deliberately or negligently disclose such confidential information to anyone other than Contractor's employees and agents with a need to know such confidential information who have agreed in writing to keep confidential the information in accordance with the terms of this Agreement. The Contractor may also disclose confidential information with the written permission of the Client or as required by law. On the request of the Client and when invoices have been paid in full to date the Contractor will promptly return all materials and documents that the Client has provided.

7. Neither party shall use or authorise others to use the name symbols or marks of the other party or that party's employees or agents in any advertising or publicity material or make any form of representation or statement that would constitute an express or implied endorsement by the other party of any commercial product or service without prior written approval from that other party whose name symbol or marks is to be used.

8. This Agreement may be terminated by either party giving thirty (30) days written notice to the other.

9. The parties to this Agreement are independent contractors. Nothing contained herein shall be deemed or construed to create between the parties hereto a partnership or joint venture or employment or principal-agent relationship. No party shall have the authority to act on behalf of any other party or to bind another party in any manner.

10. This Agreement contains the entire understanding between the parties and supersedes any previous understandings or agreements, written or otherwise, concerning this matter. It may be modified only by the written agreement of the parties.

IN WITNESS WHEREOF the parties hereto have executed this Agreement the day and year first before written. Each individual signing for a corporation hereby personally warrants his or her legal authority to bind that corporation.

Client: **Contractor:**

Name: **Name:**
_____   _____

Title: **Title:**
_____   _____

SCHEDULE "A"
SCOPE OF SERVICES

Fully detail the specifications of the project you are being contracted to complete here.

ADDENDUM TO CONTRACT

This document is in reference to the _____ agreement dated XX DATE XX, between the parties named below.

Be it known that the undersigned parties, for good consideration, agree to make the changes and/or additions outlined below. These additions shall be as valid as if part of the original contract.

No other terms or conditions of the contract are negated or changed as a result of this addendum.

YOUR NAME _____   DATE _____

YOUR SIGNATURE _____

CLIENT NAME _____   DATE _____

CLIENT SIGNATURE _____

Mutual Release From Contract

This mutual release from contract, executed on _____DATE_____ between _____CLIENT NAME / COMPANY NAME_____ of _____CLIENT ADDRESS_____, and _____YOUR NAME / COMPANY NAME_____   `.
of _____YOUR ADDRESS_____ is intended to effect the elimination of any previously agreed to contractual obligations by either party as hereinafter designated.

Whereas, disputes and differences have arisen between the parties with respect to that certain contract entered into by said parties and executed on _____DATE ORIGINAL CONTRACT WAS SIGNED_____ , a copy of which is attached hereto as Exhibit A, both parties have agreed to settle said disputes and differences by executing this mutual release.

Whereas, both parties recognize that by the execution of this mutual release, they are relinquishing their respective legal rights with reference to the herein mentioned disputes and differences, both parties agree that in consideration of this execution of this mutual release, and for the added consideration of the payment of (amount) Dollars, _____FINAL INVOICE TOTAL OR JUDGEMENT AMOUNT_____ by _____CLIENT NAME / COMPANY NAME_____ to _____YOUR NAME / COMPANY NAME_____ , receipt of which is hereby acknowledged. And the return of _____CLIENT FILES, PROJECTS, PASSWORDS, ETC_____ by _____YOUR NAME / COMPANY NAME_____ to _____CLIENT NAME / COMPANY NAME_____ receipt of which is hereby acknowledged, each party expressly releases the other party from all liability for claims and/or demands which may arise from that certain contract referenced herein and attached hereto (_____ATTACH ORIGINAL CONTRACT + ANY APPLICABLE ADDENDUMS TO THIS MUTUAL RELEASE_____).

Parties undersigned do hereby agree to this MUTUAL RELEASE FROM CONTRACT.

CLIENT NAME

CLIENT COMPANY NAME

CLIENT BUSINESS ADDRESS

DATE

CLIENT SIGNATURE: _____

YOUR NAME

YOUR COMPANY NAME

YOUR BUSINESS ADDRESS

DATE

YOUR SIGNATURE: _____

CONFIDENTIALITY AGREEMENT

This Confidentiality Agreement ("Agreement") is made and effective the **[Date]** by and between **[Client]** ("Client") and **[Consultant]** ("Consultant").

1. **Confidential Information**. Client proposes to disclose certain of its confidential and proprietary information (the "Confidential Information") to Consultant. Confidential Information shall include all data, materials, products, technology, computer programs, specifications, manuals, business plans, software, marketing plans, financial information, and other information disclosed or submitted, orally, in writing, or by any other media, to Consultant by Client. Confidential Information disclosed orally shall be identified as such within five (5) days of disclosure. Nothing herein shall require Client to disclose any of its information.

2. **Consultant's Obligations**.

   A. Consultant agrees that the Confidential Information is to be considered confidential and proprietary to Client and Consultant shall hold the same in confidence, shall not use the Confidential Information other than for the purposes of its business with Client, and shall disclose it only to its officers, directors, or employees with a specific need to know. Consultant will not disclose, publish, or otherwise reveal any of the Confidential Information received from Client to any other party whatsoever except with the specific prior written authorization of Client.

   B. Confidential Information furnished in tangible form shall not be duplicated by Consultant, except for purposes of this Agreement. Upon the request of Client, Consultant shall return all Confidential Information received in written or tangible form, including copies, or reproductions or other media containing such Confidential Information, within ten (10) days of such request. At Consultant's option, any documents or other media developed by the Consultant containing Confidential Information may be destroyed by Consultant. Consultant shall provide a written certificate to Client regarding destruction within ten (10) days thereafter.

3. **Term**. The obligations of Consultant herein shall be effective **[Non-Disclosure Period]** from the date Client last discloses any Confidential Information to Consultant pursuant to this Agreement. Further, the obligation not to disclose shall not be affected by bankruptcy, receivership, assignment, attachment or seizure procedures, whether initiated by or against Consultant, nor by the rejection of any agreement between Client and Consultant, by a trustee of Consultant in bankruptcy, or by the Consultant as a debtor-in-possession or the equivalent of any of the foregoing under local law.

4. **Other Information**. Consultant shall have no obligation under this Agreement with respect to Confidential Information which is or becomes publicly available without breach of this Agreement by Consultant; is rightfully received by Consultant without obligations of confidentiality; or is developed by Consultant without breach of this Agreement; provided, however, such Confidential Information shall not be disclosed until thirty (30) days after written notice of intent to disclose is given to Client along with the asserted grounds for disclosure.

5. **No License**. Nothing contained herein shall be construed as granting or conferring any rights by license or otherwise in any Confidential Information. It is understood and agreed that neither party solicits any change in the organization, business practice, service or products of the other party, and that the disclosure of Confidential Information shall not be construed as evidencing any intent by a party to purchase any products or services of the other party nor as an encouragement to expend funds in development or research efforts. Confidential Information may pertain to prospective or unannounced products. Consultant agrees not to use any Confidential Information as a basis upon which to develop or have a third party develop a competing or similar product.

6. **No Publicity**. Consultant agrees not to disclose its participation in this undertaking, the existence or terms and conditions of the Agreement, or the fact that discussions are being held with Client.

7. **Governing Law and Equitable Relief.** This Agreement shall be governed and construed in accordance with the laws of the United States and the State of **[State of Governing Law]** and Consultant consents to the exclusive jurisdiction of the state courts and U.S. federal courts located there for any dispute arising out of this Agreement. Consultant agrees that in the event of any breach or threatened breach by Consultant, Client may obtain, in addition to any other legal remedies which may be available, such equitable relief as may be necessary to protect Client against any such breach or threatened breach.

8. **Final Agreement**. This Agreement terminates and supersedes all prior understandings or agreements on the subject matter hereof. This Agreement may be modified only by a further writing that is duly executed by both parties.

9. **No Assignment**. Consultant may not assign this Agreement or any interest herein without Client's express prior written consent.

10. **Severability**. If any terms of this Agreement is held by a court of competent jurisdiction to be invalid or unenforceable, then this Agreement, including all of the remaining terms, will remain in full force and effect as if such invalid or unenforceable term had never been included.

11. **Notices**. Any notice required by this Agreement or given in connection with it, shall be in writing and shall be given to the appropriate party by personal delivery or by certified mail, postage prepaid, or recognized overnight delivery services.

If to Client:

[Client] [Client's Address]

If to Consultant:

[Consultant] [Consultant's Address]

12. **No Implied Waiver.** Either party's failure to insist in any one or more instances upon strict performance by the other party of any of the terms of this Agreement shall not be construed as a waiver of any continuing or subsequent failure to perform or delay in performance of any term hereof.

13. **Headings**. Headings used in this Agreement are provided for convenience only and shall not be used to construe meaning or intent.

IN WITNESS WHEREOF, the parties have executed this Agreement as of the date first above written.

Client Signature:
Consultant Signature:

**SINGLE-MEMBER
OPERATING AGREEMENT
OF
[COMPANY NAME]**

**LIMITED LIABILITY COMPANY
STATE OF [YOUR STATE]**

THIS OPERATING AGREEMENT is hereby established, this the _____ day of [use the date registered with the State]_____, 20__, by _____ the Initial Member.

The Initial Member contemplates that additional Members may join the limited liability company in the future, and the following Operating Arrangement has therefore been developed.

**ARTICLE I
FORMATIONS OF LIMITED LIABILITY COMPANY**

1. <u>Formation of LLC.</u>   The Initial Member has formed a limited liability company in the State of _____ named _____ ("LLC"). The operation of the LLC shall be governed by the terms of this Arrangement and the applicable law of the State of _____relating to the formation, operation and taxation of a LLC. To the extent permitted by law, the terms and provision of this Arrangement shall control if there is a conflict between state law and this Arrangement. The LLC shall be taxed as a sole proprietorship until and unless additional Members are added, after which the LLC will be taxed as a partnership. Any provisions of this Arrangement that may cause the LLC not to be taxed as a sole proprietorship or partnership shall be inoperative.

2. <u>Articles of Organization.</u>   The Initial Member has caused to be filed the Articles of Organization, ("Articles") of record with the state, thereby creating the LLC.

3. <u>Business.</u> The business of the LLC shall be:

   and _____ [description of your product or services]_____

   a) To conduct or promote any lawful businesses or purposes that a limited liability company is legally allowed to conduct or promote within the state or any other jurisdiction.

4. <u>Registered Office and Registered Agent.</u>The registered office and place of business of the LLC shall be __[your physical address, no PO boxes]__, and the registered agent at such office shall be _____. The registered office and/or registered agent may be changed from time to time.

5. Duration. The LLC will commence business as of the date of filing its Articles and will continue in perpetuity.

6. Fiscal Year. The LLC's fiscal and tax year shall end December 31.

ARTICLE II
MEMBERS

7. Initial Member. The Initial Member of the LLC is _____.

8. Additional Members. The first new member, or new Members if several are to be added simultaneously, may be admitted only upon approval of the Initial Member. Following the addition of a Member or Members, further new Members may be admitted only upon the consent of a majority of the existing Members and upon compliance with the provisions of this Arrangement.

ARTICLE III
MANAGEMENT

9. Management. The Initial Member shall manage the LLC, and shall have authority to take all necessary and proper actions to conduct the business of the LLC. Anyone authorized by the Initial Member may take any authorized action on behalf of the LLC.

ARTICLE IV
CONTRIBUTIONS, PROFITS, LOSSES, AND DISTRIBUTIONS

10. Interest of Member   Each Member shall own a percentage interest (sometimes referred to as a share) in the LLC. The Member's percentage interest shall be based on the amount of cash or other property that the Member has contributed to the LLC and the percentage interest shall control the Member's share of the profits, losses, and distributions of the LLC.

11. Initial Contribution. The initial contribution of the Initial Member is $_____, representing a 100% interest in the LLC.

12. Additional Contributions. In the event additional Members are added, upon a majority vote, the Members may be called upon to make additional cash contributions as may be necessary to carry on the LLC's business. The amount of any additional cash contribution shall be based on the Member's then existing percentage interest. To the extent a Member is unable to meet a cash call, the other Members can contribute the unmet call on a pro rata basis based on the Members' percentage interests at that time, and the percentage interest of each Member will be adjusted accordingly.

13. <u>Record of Contributions/Percentage Interests.</u> A record shall be kept of all contributions to, and percentage interests in, the LLC. This Arrangement, any amendment(s) to this Arrangement, and all Resolutions of the Members of the LLC shall constitute the record of the Members of the LLC and their respective interest therein.

14. <u>Profit and Losses.</u> The profits and losses and all other tax attributes of the LLC shall be allocated to the Initial Member until such time as additional Members are added at which time, the profits and losses and all other tax attributes of the LLC shall be allocated to the Members on the basis of the Members' percentage interests in the LLC.

15. <u>Distributions.</u> Any Distributions of cash or other assets of the LLC (other than in dissolution of the LLC) shall be made in the total amounts and at the times as determined by the Initial Member. Should additional Members be added, distributions of cash or other assets of the LLC (other than in dissolution of the LLC) shall be made in the total amounts and at the times as determined by a majority of the Members. Any such distributions shall be allocated among the Members on the basis of the Members' percentage interests in the LLC.

16. <u>Change in Interests.</u> In the event additional Members are added, and if during any year there is a change in a Member's percentage interest, the Member's share of profits and losses and distributions in that year shall be determined under a method which takes into account the varying interests during the year.

ARTICLE V
VOTING; CONSENT TO ACTION

17. <u>Voting by Members.</u> Until such time as additional Members are added, all decisions will be made by the Initial Member. Should additional Members be added, each Member shall be entitled to vote on any matter voted on by the Members. Voting shall be based on the percentage interest owned by each Member. The action may be taken with or without a meeting.

18. <u>Majority Defined.</u> As used throughout this agreement the term "majority" of the Members shall mean a majority of the ownership interest of the LLC as determined by the records of the LLC on the date of the action. For example, if one Member with a 51% interest votes for passage, and five members with a combined 49% interest vote against passage, the majority has voted for passage because 51% of the ownership interest has voted for passage.
Similarly, a reference to a percentage of the Members, for example: "75% of the Members," shall mean a percentage of the ownership interest of the LLC.

19. <u>Majority Required.</u> Should additional Members be added, any action that requires the vote or consent of the Members may be taken upon a majority vote of the Members, based on the Members' percentage interests unless unanimous consent is required by this Arrangement.

20. <u>Meetings – Written Consent.</u> Action of the Member or Officers may be accomplished with or without a meeting. If a meeting is held, evidence of the action shall be by Minutes or Resolution reflecting the action of the Meeting, signed by a majority of the Members, or the President and Secretary. Action without a meeting may be evidenced by a written consent signed by a majority of the Members.

21. <u>Meetings.</u> Meetings of the Members shall be held as determined by the Members or as may be called by a majority of the Members, or if a Manager was selected, then by the Manager of the LLC, or if Officers were elected or appointed, by any officer.

ARTICLE VI
DISSOCIATION OF MEMBERS

22. <u>Termination of Membership.</u> A Member's interest in the LLC shall cease upon the occurrence of one or more of the following events:

(a) A Member withdraws by giving the LLC thirty (30) days written notice in advance of the withdrawal date. Withdrawal by a Member is not a breach of this Arrangement.

(b) A Member assigns <u>all</u> of his/her interest (and not merely a partial interest) to a qualified third party.

(c) A Member dies.

(d) There is an entry of an order by a court of competent jurisdiction adjudicating the Member incompetent to manage his/her person or his/her estate.

(e) In the case of an estate that is a Member, the distribution by the fiduciary of the estate's interest in the LLC

(f) In the case of an entity that is a Member, the distribution upon dissolution of the entity's entire interest in the LLC.

(g) A Member, without the consent of a majority of the Members: (1) makes an assignment for the benefit of creditors; (2) files a voluntary petition in bankruptcy; (3) is adjudicated a bankrupt or insolvent; (4) files a petition or answer seeking for himself any reorganization, arrangement, composition, readjustment, liquidation, dissolution, or similar relief under any statute, law or regulation; (5) files an answer or other pleading admitting or failing to contest the material allegation of a petition filed against him in any proceeding of the nature described in this paragraph; (6) seeks, consents to, or acquiesces in the appointment of a trustee, receiver, or liquidator of the Member or of all or any substantial part of his properties; or (7) if any creditor permitted by law to do so should commence foreclosure or take any other action to seize or sell any Member's interest in the LLC.

(h) If within one hundred twenty (120) days after the commencement of any action against a Member seeking reorganization, arrangement, composition, readjustment, liquidation, dissolution, or similar relief under any statute, law or regulation, the action has not been dismissed and/or has not been consented to by a majority of the Members.

(i) If within ninety (90) days after the appointment, without a Member's consent or acquiescence, of a trustee, receiver, or liquidator of the Member or of all or any substantial part of the Member's properties, said appointment is not vacated or within ninety (90) days after the expiration of any stay, the appointment is not vacated and/or has not been consented to by a majority of the Members.

(j) Any of the events provided in applicable provisions of state or federal law that are not inconsistent with the dissociation events identified above.

23. <u>Effect of Dissociation.</u> Any dissociated Member shall not be entitled to receive the fair value of his LLC interest solely by virtue of his dissociation. A dissociated Member that still owns interest in the LLC shall be entitled to continue to receive such profits and losses, to receive such distribution or distributions, and to receive such allocations of income, gain, loss, deduction, credit or similar items to which he would have been entitled if still a Member. For all other purposes, a dissociated Member shall no longer be considered a Member and shall have not rights as a Member.

ARTICLE VII
RESTRICTIONS ON TRANSFERABILITY OF AN LLC INTEREST;
SET PRICE FOR LLC INTEREST

24. <u>LLC Interest.</u> The LLC interest is personal property. A Member has no interest in property owned by the LLC.

25. <u>Encumbrance.</u> A Member can encumber his LLC interest by a security interest or other form of collateral only with the consent of a majority of the other Members. Such consent shall only be given if the proceeds of the encumbrance are contributed to the LLC to respond to a cash call of the LLC.

26. <u>Sale of Interest.</u> A Member can sell his LLC interest only as follows:

(a) If a Member desires to sell his/her interest, in whole or in part, he/she shall give written notice to the LLC of his desire to sell all or part of his/her interest and must first offer the interest to the LLC. The LLC shall have the option to buy the offered interest at the then existing Set Price as provided in this Arrangement. The LLC shall have thirty (30) days from the receipt of the assigning Member's notice to give the assigning Member written notice of its intention to buy all, some, or none of the offered interest. The decision to buy shall be made by a majority of the other Members. Closing on the sale shall occur within sixty (60) days from the date that the LLC gives written notice of its intention to buy. The purchase price shall be paid in cash at closing unless the total purchase price is in excess of $_____ in which event the purchase price shall be paid in _____(_____) equal quarterly installments beginning with the date of the closing. The installment amounts shall be computed by applying the following interest factor to the principal amount: interest compounded quarterly at the Quarterly Federal Short-Term Rate existing at closing under the Applicable Federal Rates used for purposes of Internal Revenue Code § 1274(d), or any successor provision.

(b) To the extent the LLC does not buy the offered interest of the selling Member, the other Members shall have the option to buy the offered interest at the Set Price on a pro rata basis based on the Members' percentage interests at that time. If Member does not desire to buy up his/her proportional part, the other Members can buy the remaining interest on the same pro rata basis. Members shall have fifteen (15) days from the date the LLC gives its written notice to the selling Member to give the selling Member notice in writing of their intention to buy all, some, or none of the offered interest. Closing on the sales shall occur within sixty (60) days from the date that the Members give written notice of their intention to buy. The purchase price from each purchasing Member shall be paid in cash at closing.

(c) To the extent the LLC or Members do not buy the offered interest, the selling Member an then assign the interest to a non-Member. The selling Member must close on the assignment within ninety (90) days of the date that he gave notice to the LLC. If he does not close by that time, he must again give the notice and options to the LLC and the LLC Member before he sells the interest.

(d) The selling Member must close on the assignment within ninety (90) days of the date that he gave notice to the LLC. If he does not close by that time, he must again give the notice and options to the LLC and the LLC Members before he sells the interest.

(e) A non-Member purchase of a Member's interest cannot exercise any rights of a Member unless a majority of the non-selling Members consent to him becoming a Member. The non-Member purchaser will be entitled, however, to share in such profits and losses, to receive such distributions, and to receive such allocation of income, gain, loss, deduction, credit or similar items to which the selling Member would be entitled, to the extent of the interest assigned, and will be subject to calls for contributions under the terms of this Arrangement. The purchaser, by purchasing the selling Member's interest agrees to be subject to all the terms of this Arrangement as if he were a Member.

27. <u>Set Price.</u> The Set Price for purposes of this Arrangement shall be the price fixed by consent of a majority of the Members. The Set Price shall be memorialized and made part of the LLC records. The initial Set Price for each Member's interest is the amount of the Member's contribution(s) to the LLC, as updated in accordance with the terms hereof. Any future changes in the Set Price by the Members shall be based upon net equity in the assets of the LLC (fair market value of the assets less outstanding indebtedness), considering the most recent appraisal obtained by the LLC for its assets, as may be adjusted by the Members in their discretion. The initial Set Price shall be adjusted upon demand by a Member, but not more than once a year, unless all Members consent. This basis for determining the Set Price shall remain in effect until changed by consent of a majority of the Members. The Members will consider revising the basis for determining the Set Price at least annually.

ARTICLE VIII
OBLIGATION TO SELL ON DISSOCIATION
EVENT CONCERNING A MEMBER

28. <u>Dissociation.</u> Except as otherwise provided, upon the occurrence of a dissociation event with respect to a Member, the LLC and the remaining Members shall have the option to purchase the dissociated Member's interest at the Set Price in the same manner as provided herein and as if the dissociated Member had notified the LLC of his desire to sell

all of his LLC interest. The date the LLC received the notice as provided herein triggering the options shall be deemed to be the date the LLC receives actual notice of the dissociation event.

ARTICLE IX
DISSOLUTION

29. Termination of LLC. The LLC will be dissolved and its affairs must be wound up only upon such a decision by the Initial Member, provided no new Members have been added, or upon the written consent of seventy-five percent (75%) of all Members should additional Members be added.

30. Final Distributions. Upon the winding up of the LLC, the assets must be distributed as follows: (a) to the LLC creditors; (b) to Members in satisfaction of liabilities for distributions; and (c) to Members first for the return of their contributions and secondly respecting their LLC interest, in the proportions in which the Members share in profits and losses.

ARTICLE X
TAX MATTERS

31. Capital Accounts. Capital accounts shall be maintained consistent with Internal Revenue Code § 704 and the regulations thereunder.

32. Sole Proprietorship/Partnership Election. The Initial Member elects that the LLC be taxed as a sole proprietorship, and that if additional Members are admitted, the LLC be taxed as a partnership. Any provisions of the Arrangement that may cause the LLC not to be taxed as a sole proprietorship or partnership shall be inoperative.

ARTICLE XI
RECORDS AND INFORMATION

33. Records and Inspection. The LLC shall maintain at its place of business the Articles of Organization, any amendments thereto, this Arrangement, and all other LLC records required to be kept by applicable law, and the same shall be subject to inspection and copying at the reasonable request, and the expense, of any Member.

34. Obtaining Additional Information. Subject to reasonable standards, each Member may obtain from the LLC from time to time upon reasonable demand for any purpose reasonably related to the Member's interest as a Member in the LLC: (1) information regarding the state of the business and financial condition of the LLC; (2) promptly after becoming available, a copy of the LLC's federal, state, and local income tax returns for each year; and (3) other information regarding the affairs of the LLC as is just and reasonable.

ARTICLE XII
MISCELLANEOUS PROVISIONS

35. <u>Amendment.</u> Except as otherwise provided in this Arrangement, any amendment to this Arrangement may be proposed by a Member. Unless waived by the Members, the proposing Member shall submit to the Members any such proposed amendment together with an opinion of counsel as to the legality of such amendment and the recommendation of the Member as to its adoption. A proposed amendment shall become effective at such time as it has been approved in writing by a majority of the Members. This Arrangement may not be amended nor may any rights hereunder be waived except by an instrument in writing signed by the party sought to be charged with such amendment or waiver, except as otherwise provided in this Arrangement.

36. <u>Applicable Law.</u> To the extent permitted by law, this Arrangement shall be construed in accordance with and governed by the laws of the State of _____.

37. <u>Pronouns, Etc.</u> References to a Member or Manager, including by use of a pronoun, shall be deemed to include masculine, feminine, singular, plural, individuals, partnerships, corporations or other business entities, where applicable.

38. <u>Counterparts.</u> This instrument may be executed in any number of counterparts each of which shall be considered an original.

39. <u>Specific Performance.</u> Each Member agrees with the other Members that the other Members would be irreparably damaged if any of the provisions of this Arrangement are not performed in accordance with their specific terms and that monetary damages would not provide an adequate remedy in such event. Accordingly, it is agreed that, in addition to any other remedy to which the non-breaching Members may be entitled, at law or in equity, the non-breaching Members shall be entitled to injunctive relief to prevent breaches of this Arrangement and, specifically, to enforce the terms and provisions of this Arrangement in any action instituted in any court of the United States or any state thereof having subject matter jurisdiction thereof.

40. <u>Further Action.</u> Each Member, upon the request of the LLC, agrees to perform all further acts and to execute, acknowledge and deliver any documents which may be necessary, appropriate, or desirable to carry out the provisions of this Arrangement.

41. <u>Method of Notice.</u> All written notices required or permitted by this Arrangement shall be hand delivered or sent by registered or certified mail, potage prepaid, addressed to the LLC at its place of business or to a Member as set forth on the Member's signature page of this Arrangement (except that any Member may from time to time give notice changing his address for that purpose), and shall be effective when personally delivered or, if mailed, on the date set forth on the receipt of registered or certified mail.

42. <u>Facsimiles.</u> For purposes of this Arrangement, any copy, facsimile, telecommunications or other reliable reproduction of a writing, transmission or signature may be substituted or used

in lieu of the original writing, transmission or signature for any and all purposes for which the original writing, transmission or signature could be used, provided such copy, facsimile telecommunication or other reproduction shall have been confirmed received by the sending Party.

43. Computation of Time. In computing any period of time under this Arrangement, the day of the act, event or default from which designated period of time begins to run shall not be included. The last day of the period so computed shall be included, unless it is a Saturday, Sunday or legal holiday, in which event the period shall run until the end of the next day which is not a Saturday, Sunday or legal holiday.

WHEREFORE, the Initial Member, being the single Member of this LLC, has executed this Arrangement on the _____ day of _____, 20__.

Signed:_____
                [Initial Member's Name]
                [Initial Member's SSN]
                [Initial Member's Address]
                [Initial Member's City, State, Zip]

PARTNERSHIP AGREEMENT

THIS PARTNERSHIP AGREEMENT is made this _____ day of _____, 20__, by and between the following individuals:

_____ Address: _____

City/State/ZIP:_____

_____ Address: _____

City/State/ZIP:_____

1. <u>Nature of Business</u>. The partners listed above hereby agree that they shall be considered partners in business for the following purpose:

_____

_____

2. <u>Name.</u> The partnership shall be conducted under the name of _____ and shall maintain offices at [STREET ADDRESS], [CITY, STATE, ZIP].

3. <u>Day-To-Day Operation.</u> The partners shall provide their full-time services and best efforts on behalf of the partnership. No partner shall receive a salary for services rendered to the partnership. Each partner shall have equal rights to manage and control the partnership and its business. Should there be differences between the partners concerning ordinary business matters, a decision shall be made by unanimous vote. It is understood that the partners may elect one of the partners to conduct the day-to-day business of the partnership; however, no partner shall be able to bind the partnership by act or contract to any liability exceeding $_____ without the prior written consent of each partner.

4. <u>Capital Contribution.</u> The capital contribution of each partner to the partnership shall consist of the following property, services, or cash which each partner agrees to contribute:

Name Of Partner	Capital Contribution	Agreed-Upon Cash	% Share

The partnership shall maintain a capital account record for each partner; should any partner's capital account fall below the agreed to amount, then that partner shall (1) have his share of partnership profits then due and payable applied instead to his capital account; and (2) pay any deficiency to the partnership if his share of partnership profits is not yet due and payable or, if it is, his share is insufficient to cancel the deficiency.

5. <u>Profits and Losses.</u> The profits and losses of the partnership shall be divided by the partners according to a mutually agreeable schedule and at the end of each calendar year according to the proportions listed above.

6. <u>Term/Termination.</u> The term of this Agreement shall be for a period of ____ years, unless the partners mutually agree in writing to a shorter period. Should the partnership be terminated by unanimous vote, the assets and cash of the partnership shall be used to pay all creditors, with the remaining amounts to be distributed to the partners according to their proportionate share.

7. <u>Disputes.</u> This Partnership Agreement shall be governed by the laws of the State of _____. Any disputes arising between the partners as a result of this Agreement shall be settled by arbitration in accordance with the rules of the American Arbitration Association and judgment upon the award rendered may be entered in any court having jurisdiction thereof.

8. <u>Withdrawal/Death of Partner.</u> In the event a partner withdraws or retires from the partnership for any reason, including death, the remaining partners may continue to operate the partnership using the same name. A withdrawing partner shall be obligated to give sixty (60) days' prior written notice of his/her intention to withdraw or retire and shall be obligated to sell his/her interest in the partnership. No partner shall transfer interest in the partnership to any other party without the written consent of the remaining partner(s). The remaining partner(s) shall pay the withdrawing or retiring partner, or to the legal representative of the deceased or disabled partner, the value of his interest in the partnership, or (a) the sum of his capital account, (b) any unpaid loans due him, (c) his proportionate share of accrued net profits remaining undistributed in his capital account, and (d) his interest in any prior agreed appreciation in the value of the partnership property over its book value. No value for good will shall be included in determining the value of the partner's interest.

9. <u>Non-Compete Agreement.</u> A partner who retires or withdraws from the partnership shall not directly or indirectly engage in a business which is or which would be competitive with the existing or then anticipated business of the partnership for a period of _____, in those _____ of this State where the partnership is currently doing or planning to do business.

IN WITNESS WHEREOF, the partners have duly executed this Agreement on the day and year set forth hereinabove.

_____ Partner   _____ Partner

PARTNERSHIP DISSOLUTION AGREEMENT

By signing this agreement ("Agreement") the Partners of **{name of Partnership and/or business),** henceforth known as "Partnership" acknowledge and consent to dissolving said Partnership on the **{date}** of **{month}**, **{year}**.

The names of the Partners in this Partnership are as follows:

{list of names of Partners}

The previously listed Partners undersign this Agreement and acknowledge and agree to the following provisions:

LIQUIDATING PARTNER. The Partners agree that **{Name}** will be named the "Liquidating Partner." As such, **{Name}** will be responsible for **{details on what is expected from the Liquidating Partner, including determining liabilities and assets, distributing the assets, dealing with taxes, etc.}**. Partners may also mutually agree upon a separate representative to act on their behalf in this matter.

SELLING PARTNER. {If this is not a complete dissolution of the Partnership, and only one partner, or some of the partners, are leaving, here is where you enter information on who the selling partner is, who will be purchasing the selling partner's interest, what the cost of the interest is, etc.}.

INVENTORY. The Liquidating Partner, or other representative agreed upon by the Partners, will be responsible for determining the extent of the inventory, if any, of the Partnership. Liquidating Partner or representative will also be responsible for determining what will become of the inventory. Liquidating Partner has the right to sell and/or otherwise distribute the inventory, particularly if doing so will allow Partnership to diminish its liabilities and/or debts.

STATEMENT OF ACCOUNT. Liquidating Partner, or other representative, will provide all Partners with a Statement of Account for the Partnership. Said Statement will include a complete list of inventory, as well as any assets, liabilities, and/or debts belonging to the company. Statement of Account will become a matter of record in the Partnership's books, and Partners may access said books according to the rules listed in the original Partnership Agreement.

ALLOCATION OF LIABILITIES AND/OR DEBTS. Liquidating Partner, or other representative, shall determine, through the course of evaluating inventory and completing the Statement of Account, any liabilities and/or debts the Partnership has incurred. Liquidating Partner, or other representative, shall then use the appropriate means to rectify said liabilities and/or assets. If there is a provision in the original Partnership Agreement for this procedure, Liquidating Partner must follow that Agreement. If not, Liquidating Partner, by virtue of his/her position, has the right to take care of any liabilities and/or debts in the most efficient and positive manner possible for the Partnership.

DISTRIBUTION OF ASSETS. Liquidating Partner, or other representative, will distribute the assets, less any liabilities or debts, to the Partners in the manner established by the original Partnership Agreement. If no such provision was included in the Partnership Agreement, Partners must agree to a method for distribution. If no agreement is possible, Partners agree to take the matter to a third-party arbitrator for settlement.

TAX OBLIGATIONS. Liquidating Partner, or other representative, shall determine the tax obligations of the Partnership and/or the Partners. Liquidating Partner, or other representative, shall then prepare and file all required tax forms and/or returns.

RELEASE. Each Partner releases all other partners from any and all known claims, actions, and demands arising as a result of the Partnership. Release does not prevent a Partner from bringing suit under this Dissolution Agreement, should this Agreement not be fulfilled according to the rules set forth.

INDEMNIFICATION. Partners agree to indemnify and hold harmless the Liquidating Partner from claims, damages, or obligations of any kind with regard to his/her duties in liquidating this Partnership, unless claims or losses come as a result of the Liquidating Partner's breach of contract and/or unethical behavior.

DISPUTES. Should the Partners have any disputes with regard to this Agreement, **{description of what will be done, such as seeking a third party arbitrator}**.

SEVERABILITY. If one or more sections of this Agreement are declared invalid, those sections are null and void, but all other sections remain enforceable.

JURISDICTION. This Agreement is bound by the laws and regulations of the State of **{State Name}**.

By signing below, the Partners agree to dissolve {Name of Partnership} freely and willingly, according to the terms listed above.

Signed this {date} of {month}, {year} by:

_____   _____
Partner Name   Partner Name

_____   _____
Partner Signature   Partner Signature

_____   _____
Partner Name   Partner Name

_____   _____
Partner Signature   Partner Signature

WEBSITE DESIGN CONTRACT

Set forth this **{date}** day of **{month}**, **{year}**, this agreement ("Agreement") is entered into between **{Client Name}**, known for the purpose of this Agreement as "Client," and **{Designer Name}**, hereafter known as "Designer." The Agreement refers to the following website design project(s) (hereafter referred to as "Work"):

**{Detailed description of the website design project(s)
that applies to this Agreement}**

Client and Designer agree to the following provisions:

DURATION: This Agreement commences on the day listed above, and continues through the **{date}** of **{month}**, **{year}**, at which point all Work is expected to be completed to Client's satisfaction. Extensions may be requested by Designer, and granted or denied by the Client.

PAYMENT: Client agrees to pay Designer **{amount of payment}** for **{description of Work expected for this payment, represented in hours, amount of Work, or some other measure}**. Payment is due **{date and/or payment schedule}**.

ADDITIONAL PAYMENT: Client agrees to pay Designer's expenses for **{expenses agreed upon by Client and Designer}**, assuming the Designer provides proper documentation (e.g., receipts).

CHANGES: Any changes made to the original description as outlined above will result in Designer charging additional fees of **{amount of money}** per **{hour, day, week, project, etc.}**. Should Designer request and Client agree to an extension of time, Client {will/will not} pay Designer additional funds at the same rate for the completion of the project, and the parties will draw up an agreement to that effect.

CLIENT RESPONSIBILITIES: Client agrees to provide Designer with **{Designer's requirements}** so that the Work may be completed on time and to Client's satisfaction.

CONFIDENTIALITY: Client and Designer agree to discuss the Work listed above with only one another and any other agreed upon parties, listed here: **{any parties allowed access to the information, property and/or materials involved in the Work}**. Confidentiality applies to **{what is considered to be protected by this Agreement}**, and continues until **{length of time that each party is to keep confidential anything listed here}**.

RIGHTS: Rights, including copyright, ownership, and publishing rights, to this Work belong to **{Client/Company}** as of **{Date}**, through **{Date}**, upon which point they will **{transfer to the other party, become public domain, etc.}**.

RELATIONSHIP: This Agreement does not imply any other relationship between Client and Designer. Any further Work requested by Client and/or suggested by Designer must be governed under a separate agreement.

This undersigned consent to all the provisions in this Agreement, signed this **{date}** day of **{month}**, **{year}**.

_____ _____

Designer Name Client Name

_____ _____

Designer Signature Client Signature

Project Management Contract

1. _____ (hereafter " Contractor") agrees to provide the following products and services to _____ (hereafter "Client"):

_____

_____

This work will be completed no later than **MM/DD/YYYY**, and will be conducted by Contractors' agent, _____.

The parties agree that circumstances arising during the course of this contract may require changes to the products and services described above. The parties agree to negotiate any such changes and Contractor's remuneration for them in good faith, set them in writing, and incorporate them into this contract as an attachment.

2. Client agrees to:

   A. participate as requested in activities necessary to Contractor's fulfillment of his obligations, including

   _____

   B. pay Contractor a fee not to exceed **$X** plus expenses. Expenses to be billed include travel (**$0.XX** per mile for auto travel), lodging and meals attendant to Contractor's work on Client's behalf, long-distance phone calls, and any copying and mailing services, outside of normal communication with Client. Lodging and meal expenses will be documented with receipts.

   The payments will be made in three installments: **$X** at the signing of this contract; **$X** upon completion of _____ described above; and **$X** upon completion of this project. The project will be considered complete when _____ described above is completed.

2. Either Party may terminate this agreement with **X** days' written notice. If the agreement is terminated, Contractor will present Client with a statement of account showing all fees paid to that time, and itemizing work performed. If work performed exceeds fees paid to date, Client will pay Contractor for such work at the rate of **$X**. If fees paid exceed work performed to date, Contractor will return unearned fees to Client.

In witness to their agreement to the terms of this contract, the parties affix their signatures below:

_____   _____
Client, signature & date   Contractor, signature & date

Address_____   Address_____

City, state, ZIP_____   City, state, ZIP _____

GHOSTWRITER AGREEMENT

This agreement ("Agreement") is between **{Name}**, henceforth referred to as "Author," and **{Name}**, henceforth referred to as "Ghostwriter," and is executed this **{date}** day of **{month}**, **{year}**.

Author and Ghostwriter are entering into this Agreement for the purposes of completing **{description of book and/or other publication covered under this Agreement, including working title and estimated length}**, herein referred to as the "Work." As such, Author and Ghostwriter agree to the following provisions:

Method. In order to accomplish the Work, Ghostwriter will **{description of how Author and Ghostwriter intend to work together, including any mandatory meetings, times Ghostwriter is expected to work, etc.}**.

Plagiarism. Ghostwriter agrees that all Work created for Author is **{his/her}** own unique work, and does not borrow from any other copyrighted work.

Deadline. Ghostwriter will have **{amount}** of the Work done by **{deadline date}**. **{include additional deadlines here, and explain if Author will have access to the Work at any point during the writing process}**.

Payment. Payment for the Work will be delivered according to the following schedule: **{outline the payment plan. Is Ghostwriter getting an advance, money at the halfway point, etc.?}**.

Royalties. Ghostwriter will not be entitled to any royalties, residuals, or commissions upon the sale of the work. Total payment for Ghostwriter is **{amount in dollars}**, payable according to the terms listed above.

Copyrights. Author will own the Work, including any copyrights and sale or distribution rights.

Credit. Credit for the Work will **{indicate if Author will be the only credit on the book, or if there will be an "as told to" or "with" credit for Ghostwriter}**.

Confidentiality. Ghostwriter acknowledges that **{he/she}** will have access to certain privileged information during the course of this project. Ghostwriter agrees to keep all information confidential from any and all third parties, during and after the course of this project.

Termination. Author **{will/will not}** have the right to terminate this Agreement at any point. Should Author terminate the Ghostwriter's services, Author will be required to pay Ghostwriter for completed work, according to the provisions outlined in the "Payment" section of this

Agreement. Similarly, Ghostwriter **{will/will not}** have the right to end this Agreement at any point. **{Outline any further details about this clause, including perhaps the amount of Work Ghostwriter must complete to avoid any legal recourse}.**

Author and Ghostwriter agree to the above terms, and undersign here to that effect.

_____

Author Name

_____

Ghostwriter Name

_____

Author Signature

_____

Ghostwriter Signature

CONSULTANT SERVICES AGREEMENT

This agreement dated _____DATE_____, is made By and Between _____CLIENT/COMPANY NAME_____, whose address is _____CLIENT ADDRESS_____, referred to as "Company", AND _____YOUR NAME/COMPANY NAME_____, whose address is _____YOUR ADDRESS_____, referred to as "Consultant."

1. **Consultation Services.** The company hereby employs the consultant to perform the following services in accordance with the terms and conditions set forth in this agreement: The consultant will consult with the officers and employees of the company concerning matters relating to _____FILL IN YOUR OWN SERVICE INFO HERE_____ (For example: the management and organization of the company, their financial policies, the terms and conditions of employment, and generally any matter arising out of the business affairs of the company, etc.)

2. **Terms of Agreement.** This agreement will begin _____DATE_____ and will end _____DATE_____. Either party may cancel this agreement on thirty (30) days notice to the other party in writing, by certified mail, personal delivery, or email with delivery confirmation.

3. **Time Devoted by Consultant.** It is anticipated the consultant will spend approximately ___HOURS___ (hours/weeks/months) in fulfilling the obligations laid out under this contract. The particular amount of time may vary from day to day or week to week. However, the consultant shall devote a minimum of ___HOURS___ per month to duties in accordance with this agreement.

4. **Place Where Services Will Be Rendered.** The consultant will perform most services in accordance with this contract at _____ENTER LOCATION WORK WILL GENERALLY BE PERFORMED_____ (For example: at your home office, at your client's company location/site). In addition the consultant may perform services via the telephone, email, Instant Messenger, text message, video conference, or similar, and at such other places as necessary to perform these services in accordance with this agreement.

5. **Payment to Consultant.** The consultant will be paid at the rate of $___YOUR CONSULTING RATE_____ per ____HOURS/WEEK/MONTH____ for work performed in accordance with this agreement. However, the consultant will be paid at least $___MINIMUM RETAINER AMOUNT___ per month regardless of the amount of time spent in accordance with this agreement. The consultant will submit an itemized statement setting forth the time spent and services rendered, and the company will pay the consultant the amounts due as indicated by statements submitted by the consultant within ten (10) days of receipt.

6. **Independent Contractor**. Both the company and the consultant agree that the consultant will act as an independent contractor in the performance of duties under this contract. Accordingly, the consultant shall be responsible for payment of all taxes including Federal, State and local taxes arising out of the consultant's activities in accordance with this contract, including by way of illustration but not limitation, Federal and State income tax, Social Security tax, Unemployment Insurance taxes, and any other taxes or business license fee as required.

7. **Confidential Information**. The consultant agrees that any information received by the consultant during any furtherance of the consultant's obligations in accordance with this contract, which concerns the personal, financial or other affairs of the company will be treated by the consultant in full confidence and will not be revealed to any other persons, firms or organizations.

8. **Employment of Others**. The company may from time to time request that the consultant arrange for the services of other service providers. All costs to the consultant for those services will be paid by the company, but in no event shall the consultant employ others without the prior authorization of the company.

9. **Signatures**. Both the company and the consultant agree to the above contract. Witnessed by:

Signature _____ Date _____
COMPANY
COMPANY ADDRESS
COMPANY CONTACT INFO

Signature _____ Date _____
CONSULTANT
CONSULTANT ADDRESS
CONSULTANT CONTACT INFO

YOUR BUSINESS NAME OR LOGO

Business Address
Business Phone Number
Business Email Address
Company #: {Company number}; VAT #: {VAT number}

UK Consultant Services Agreement

1. **Introduction and Definitions:**

   This Agreement is between _____ (organisation's name and address) (herein after called _____) and (_____) (herein after called 'the Consultant').

   The Agreement will be in accordance with the following Terms and Conditions unless and until an alternative is specifically agreed between the Parties.

   This agreement is made effective as of **[___ DATE ___]**

   By and between: **[___ Client Name ___]**
   CLIENT NAME / COMPANY NAME
   CLIENT ADDRESS
   CLIENT PHONE

   and **[___ Your Name / Your Company Name ___]**
   YOUR NAME / COMPANY NAME
   YOUR BUSINESS ADDRESS
   YOUR BUSINESS PHONE
   Company #: {Company number}; VAT #: {VAT number}

2. **Purpose of the Agreement:**

   The purpose of the Agreement is:
   Further details of the Agreement are set out in the attached Schedule.

3. **Commencement date and duration of the Agreement:**

   This Agreement will commence on (_____) and is to be carried out in accordance with the following conditions:
   It may be terminated by either party giving one month's notice in writing. [Organisation] may terminate the agreement immediately in the event that the Consultant commits any material breach of the terms of this Agreement, where a consultant acts negligently, or in a manner that seriously harms the reputation of [Organisation], or behaves in a way that is inconsistent with the [organisation's] disciplinary rules.

4. Fees and expenses:

Fees for the Agreement will be as follows:

Where necessary, VAT will be added at the appropriate rate.
Where appropriate, travel, subsistence and other expenses will be paid at cost and in accordance with arrangements specifically agreed, in advance, with the Consultant.

5. Invoices and payment:

Unless specifically agreed otherwise, invoices will be submitted monthly by the Consultant and payment made within 30 days.

6. Taxation:

The Consultant is a self-employed person responsible for taxation and National Insurance or similar liabilities or contributions in respect of the fees and the Consultant will indemnify [organisation] against all liability for the same and any costs, claims or expenses including interest and penalties.

7. Confidentiality:

The Consultant will not divulge to third parties matters confidential to (_____) (whether or not covered by this Agreement) without (_____) explicit permission.

Except where specifically agreed otherwise, all material, data, information, etcetera, collected during the course of the Agreement will remain in the possession of (_____) and not used without their permission.

8. Publication of material:

Where the Agreement provides for the publication of material, the following specific conditions shall apply:

(a) _____ will retain the right to edit the final draft prior to publication subject, in the case of joint publications, to amendments proposed being agreed with the author(s).

(b) prior to publication, the Consultant and/or others associated with the publication shall not disclose any material obtained or produced for the purposes of the project to any other party unless _____ have given prior approval in writing.

(c) the Consultant will provide to _____ copies of all material, data etcetera collected specifically for the project and indicate the source of other material used.

(d) _____ will, except where specifically agreed otherwise, hold copyright to the publication.

Other matters relating to the use of the material shall be covered as an Appendix to this Agreement. Where other uses are agreed, all material and publications based on the project shall acknowledge _____ .

9. Restrictions:

The Consultant shall not, whilst this Agreement is in force, be engaged or concerned directly or indirectly in the provision of services to any other party in the same or similar field of business or activity to _____ without the prior written consent of _____ .

10. Copyright/patent:

All work created, developed, invented, carried out or produced during your engagement or arising out of or in consequence of this Agreement, shall be deemed to have been made by or on behalf of [Organisation]. The work, together with the benefit of any such work, belongs exclusively to [Organisation]. You must give [Organisation] full details of all and any such work. You must, at [Organisation]'s request and cost both during the contract and thereafter, if required, take all steps as may be necessary or desirable to substantiate [Organisation]'s rights in respect of any such work.

12. Other conditions:

Any other conditions, including variations to the terms set out above, shall be included as an Appendix to this Agreement.

For _____ (Organisation)

Signed: _____

Date: _____

Name: _____

Designation: _____

For the Consultant

Signed: _____

Date: _____

Name: _____

Designation: _____

CEASE AND DESIST AGREEMENT

Pursuant to **{applicable law}**, **{Name}** agrees to immediately cease and desist **{activity, use of copyrighted marks, use of likenesses, etc.}** as of **{date}**.

{Name} agrees to discontinue any **{marketing campaigns, current websites with illegal material on them, signs bearing the illegal material, etc.}** and stop **{the illegal activity}** from being used in the future in any way, shape, or form, including any advertising, sales, or distribution.

{Name} further agrees that **{he/she/it}** has destroyed and/or will immediately destroy any remaining **{illegal material}**.

Should **{Name}** fail to accomplish any of the above tasks, **{Offended Party}** will have no choice but to seek legal recourse through whatever means available.

Signed this **{date}** day of **{month}**, **{year}**:

_____   _____
Printed Name   Printed Name

_____   _____
Signature   Signature

AGREEMENT TO PURCHASE DOMAIN NAME

This purchase AGREEMENT, made this **{date}** day of **{month}**, **{year}** between the parties **{Name of Seller}**, henceforth referred to in this AGREEMENT as Seller, and **{Name of Buyer}**, henceforth referred to in this AGREEMENT as Buyer, legally transfers sole ownership of the internet domain name **{domain name}**, henceforth referred to as PROPERTY in this AGREEMENT, from Seller to Buyer in exchange for the full AMOUNT, paid on the **{date}** of **{month}**, **{year}**, of **{amount}** (USD).

Upon the Seller's receipt of this {AMOUNT}, the Seller shall:

1. Relinquish all proprietary and intellectual rights, past, present and future in nature to the Seller, concerning the domain name above listed;

2. Maintain no copyrights or trademarks on the PROPERTY above listed;

3. Hold the Buyer harmless in any court of law from any resolved or unresolved legal disputes or copyright infringements involving the PROPERTY above listed filed prior to the date of this AGREEMENT; and

4. Make no intellectual or proprietary claim to the above listed domain name in any manner, written or verbal, in any forum, public or private; and

5. Transfer the entirety of the above listed PROPERTY to the Buyer on the **{date}** of **{month}**, **{year}**.

Upon the Seller's receipt of this AMOUNT, the Buyer shall:

1. Obtain full proprietary and intellectual rights to the PROPERTY above listed;

2. Hold harmless the Seller from any resolved or unresolved legal disputes or copyright infringements which occur after the date of this exchange AGREEMENT; and

3. Obtain full rights to legally copyright the PROPERTY at any time of the Buyer's choice.

We the undersigned agree to this legally binding AGREEMENT and fully understand the terms as set forth in said AGREEMENT.

_____ SIGNED ___/___/20____

Seller

(Print name here): _____

_____ SIGNED ___/___/20____

Buyer

(Print name here): _____

ASSIGNMENT OF COPYRIGHT

The undersigned hereby agrees to transfer, sell, or assign to **[name]** and his/her successors and representatives all rights and interests in the copyrighted works described below:

<u>TITLE</u>   <u>REGISTRATION</u>

The undersigned certifies that he/she has good title to the copyright and it is free from all liens and encumbrances. Furthermore, there are no known claims against the aforementioned copyright.

ASSIGNOR _____   DATE _____

WITNESS _____   DATE _____

32469437R00125

Made in the USA
Lexington, KY
21 May 2014